Supporting Children with Sensory impairment

This book provides a quick and easy reference guide to different types of sensory impairment, including causes, symptoms and the implications for teaching and learning. With most children and young people with hearing or visual impairments attending mainstream schools, this book explains the most effective and practical strategies for use in mainstream classrooms. Fully up to date with the 2014 SEND Code of Practice, this accessible resource is split into two parts: 'Supporting children with a hearing impairment' and 'Supporting children with a visual impairment'. The wide-ranging chapters include:

- Educational access for pupils with hearing loss
- Teaching phonics
- Teaching deaf pupils with English as a second language
- Identifying children with visual impairment
- Classroom management
- Adapting resources

This practical text provides strategies to use in schools to ensure that children with sensory impairments are fully supported. Featuring useful checklists and photocopiable resources, it contains a wealth of valuable advice and tried-and-tested strategies for teachers and support staff working in early years settings, schools, academies and colleges.

Gill Blairmires – Qualified Teacher of the Deaf, Integrated Sensory and Physical Service (IPaSS), Hull, UK

Cath Coupland – Qualified Teacher of the Visually Impaired, Integrated Sensory and Physical Service (IPaSS), Hull, UK

Tracey Galbraith – Qualified Teacher of the Visually Impaired, Integrated Sensory and Physical Service (IPaSS), Hull, UK

Jon Parker – Qualified Teacher of the Deaf (previously Head of Service), Integrated Sensory and Physical Service (IPaSS), Hull, UK

Annette Parr – Qualified Teacher of the Deaf, Integrated Sensory and Physical Service (IPaSS), Hull, UK

Fiona Simpson – Qualified Teacher of the Visually Impaired, Integrated Sensory and Physical Service (IPaSS), Hull, UK

Paul Thornton – Qualified Teacher of the Visually Impaired, Integrated Sensory and Physical Service (IPaSS), Hull, UK

Helping Everyone Achieve ■■■

nasen is a professional membership association that supports all those who work with or care for children and young people with special and additional educational needs. Members include teachers, teaching assistants, support workers, other educationalists, students and parents.

nasen supports its members through policy documents, journals, its magazine *Special,* publications, professional development courses, regional networks and newsletters. Its website contains more current information such as responses to government consultations. **nasen's** published documents are held in very high regard both in the UK and internationally.

Other titles published in association with the National Association for Special Educational Needs (nasen):

Language for Learning in the Secondary School: A practical guide for supporting students with speech, language and communication needs
Sue Hayden and Emma Jordan
2012/pb: 978-0-415-61975-2

Using Playful Practice to Communicate with Special Children
Margaret Corke
2012/pb: 978-0-415-68767-6

The Equality Act for Educational Professionals: A simple guide to disability and inclusion in schools
Geraldine Hills
2012/pb: 978-0-415-68768-3

More Trouble with Maths: A teacher's complete guide to identifying and diagnosing mathematical difficulties
Steve Chinn
2012/pb: 978-0-415-67013-5

Dyslexia and Inclusion: Classroom Approaches for Assessment, Teaching and Learning, 2ed
Gavin Reid
2012/pb: 978-0-415-60758-2

Promoting and Delivering School-to-School Support for Special Educational Needs: A practical guide for SENCOs
Rita Cheminais
2013/pb 978-0-415-63370-3

Time to Talk: Implementing outstanding practice in speech, language and communication
Jean Gross
2013/pb: 978-0-415-63334-5

Curricula for Teaching Children and Young People with Severe or Profound and Multiple Learning Difficulties: Practical strategies for educational professionals
Peter Imray and Viv Hinchcliffe
2013/pb: 978-0-415-83847-4

Successfully Managing ADHD: A handbook for SENCOs and teachers
Fintan O'Regan
2014/pb: 978-0-415-59770-8

Brilliant Ideas for Using ICT in the Inclusive Classroom, 2ed
Sally McKeown and Angela McGlashon
2015/pb: 978-1-138-80902-4

Boosting Learning in the Primary Classroom: Occupational therapy strategies that really work with pupils
Sheilagh Blyth
2015/pb: 978-1-13-882678-6

Beating Bureaucracy in Special Educational Needs, 3ed
Jean Gross
2015/pb: 978-1-138-89171-5

Transforming Reading Skills in the Secondary School: Simple strategies for improving literacy
Pat Guy
2015/pb: 978-1-138-89272-9

Supporting Children with Speech and Language Difficulties, 2ed
Cathy Allenby, Judith Fearon-Wilson, Sally Merrison and Elizabeth Morling
2015/pb: 978-1-138-85511-3

Supporting Children with Dyspraxia and Motor Co-ordination Difficulties, 2ed
Susan Coulter, Lesley Kynman, Elizabeth Morling, Rob Grayson and Jill Wing
2015/pb: 978-1-138-85507-6

Developing Memory Skills in the Primary Classroom: A complete programme for all
Gill Davies
2015/pb: 978-1-138-89262-0

Language for Learning in the Primary School: A practical guide for supporting pupils with language and communication difficulties across the curriculum, 2ed
Sue Hayden and Emma Jordan
2015/pb: 978-1-138-89862-2

Supporting Children with Autistic Spectrum Disorders, 2ed
Elizabeth Morling and Colleen O'Connell
2016/pb: 978-1-138-85514-4

Understanding and Supporting Pupils with Moderate Learning Difficulties in the Secondary School: A practical guide
Rachael Hayes and Pippa Whittaker
2016/pb: 978-1-138-01910-2

Assessing Children with Specific Learning Difficulties: A teacher's practical guide
Gavin Reid, Gad Elbeheri and John Everatt
2016/pb: 978-0-415-67027-2

Supporting Children with Down's Syndrome, 2ed
Lisa Bentley, Ruth Dance, Elizabeth Morling, Susan Miller and Susan Wong
2016/pb: 978-1-138-91485-8

Provision Mapping and the SEND Code of Practice: Making it work in primary, secondary and special schools, 2ed
Anne Massey
2016/pb: 978-1-138-90707-2

Supporting Children with Medical Conditions, 2ed
Susan Coulter, Lesley Kynman, Elizabeth Morling, Francesca Murray, Jill Wing and Rob Grayson
2016/pb: 978-1-13-891491-9

Achieving Outstanding Classroom Support in Your Secondary School: Tried and tested strategies for teachers and SENCOs.
Jill Morgan, Cheryl Jones and Sioned Booth-Coates
2016/pb: 978-1-138-83373-9

Supporting Children with Sensory Impairment
Gill Blairmires, Cath Coupland, Tracey Galbraith, Elizabeth Morling, Jon Parker, Annette Parr, Fiona Simpson and Paul Thornton
2016/pb: 978-1-138-91919-8

Supporting Children with Sensory Impairment

Gill Blairmires, Cath Coupland, Tracey Galbraith, Jon Parker, Annette Parr, Fiona Simpson and Paul Thornton

Series Editor: Elizabeth Morling

Routledge
Taylor & Francis Group

LONDON AND NEW YORK

Helping Everyone Achieve

First published 2016
by Routledge
2 Park Square, Milton Park, Abingdon, Oxon OX14 4RN

and by Routledge
711 Third Avenue, New York, NY 10017

*Routledge is an imprint of the Taylor & Francis Group,
an informa business*

British Library Cataloguing in Publication Data
A catalogue record for this book is available from the British Library

Library of Congress Cataloging-in-Publication Data
Blairmires, Gill, author.
Supporting children with sensory impairment / Gill Blairmires, Cath
Coupland, Tracey Galbraith, Elizabeth Morling, Jon Parker, Annette
Parr, Fiona Simpson & Paul Thornton.
Abingdon, Oxon ; New York : Routledge is an imprint of the Taylor &
Francis Group, an Informa Business, [2016]
LCCN 2015029620 | ISBN 9781138919242
(hardback : alk. paper) | ISBN 9781138919198 (pbk. : alk. paper) |
ISBN 9781315687940 (ebook)
Deafblind children–Education–Great Britain. | Children with
disabilities–Education–Great Britain.
LCC HV1597.2 .B535 2016 | DDC 371.910941–dc23
LC record available at http://lccn.loc.gov/2015029620

ISBN: 978-1-138-91924-2 (hbk)
ISBN: 978-1-138-91919-8 (pbk)
ISBN: 978-1-315-68794-0 (ebk)

Typeset in Helvetica
by Cenveo Publisher Services

Contents

PART B
Supporting children with a visual impairment 45

Foreword

This book is in two parts: supporting children with a hearing impairment, and supporting children with a visual impairment.

Part A: Supporting children with a hearing impairment is written by:

- Jon Parker, Qualified Teacher of the Deaf (previously Head of Service), Integrated Sensory and Physical Service (IPaSS), Hull
- Annette Parr, Qualified Teacher of the Deaf, Integrated Sensory and Physical Service (IPaSS), Hull
- Gill Blairmires, Qualified Teacher of the Deaf, Integrated Sensory and Physical Service (IPaSS), Hull.

It is produced in partnership with Hull and District Deaf Children's Society.

Part B: Supporting children with a visual impairment is written by:

- Cath Coupland, Qualified Teacher of the Visually Impaired, Integrated Sensory and Physical Service (IPaSS), Hull
- Tracey Galbraith, Qualified Teacher of the Visually Impaired, Integrated Sensory and Physical Service (IPaSS), Hull
- Fiona Simpson, Qualified Teacher of the Visually Impaired, Integrated Sensory and Physical Service (IPaSS), Hull
- Paul Thornton, Qualified Teacher of the Visually Impaired, Integrated Sensory and Physical Service (IPaSS), Hull.

It contains contributions from Dr Linda Evans.

The book is edited by Elizabeth Morling, Series Editor, SEN Consultant and former Head of the Education Service for Physical Disability, Hull City Council, UK.

This book is written for teachers and support staff in early years settings, schools, academies and colleges who are encountering pupils with hearing or visual impairment. It may also be of interest to parents of children with either of these impairments.

Most children and young people with hearing or visual impairment are educated in mainstream schools. Results gathered by the professionals in the field show that *with the correct support* their educational progress and outcomes will be good. Early intervention by professionals is a very important part of the support, preferably starting as soon as a hearing or visual impairment has been diagnosed even with very young babies. With the current development of Education Health Care Plans, support should continue into Further Education up to the age of 25.

The book identifies indicators that there is a need for support for children and young people, together with signposts and pathways that will make the learning journey a successful one, with full access to the pre-school experience or relevant curriculum.

It is expected that pupils will be referred to the specialist hearing or visually impaired support service in their area in order for them to receive the correct expertise. The support for a specific child or young person will be the result of a detailed discussion between themselves (if appropriate), professionals from the relevant support service, schools, other professionals, parents or guardians.

The word 'school' is used throughout the book but this refers to early years settings, schools and academies and colleges.

A variety of terms are used to describe those individuals whom this book is intended to support, i.e. children and young people, child or pupil.

Legislation and guidance

In order to fully meet the needs of pupils with a hearing or visual impairment, the following information should be considered.

The Special Education Needs and Disability Code of Practice, 2014 states:

> that special educational needs and provision can be considered as falling under four broad areas:
>
> 1. Communication and interaction
> 2. Cognition and learning
> 3. Social, mental and emotional health
> 4. Sensory and/or physical
>
> Many children and young people with vision impairment (VI), hearing impairment (HI) or a multi-sensory impairment (MSI) will require specialist support and/or equipment to access their learning, or habilitation support. Children and young people with an MSI have a combination of vision and hearing difficulties.
>
> (p. 98)

The above document also refers to children who have other types of learning difficulty. 'This means that they either: have a significantly greater difficulty in learning than the majority of children of the same age; or have a disability which prevents or hinders them from making use of educational facilities of a kind generally provided for children of the same age in schools within the area of the local education authority.' This statement clearly refers to those with a hearing or visual impairment.

The Equality Act 2010 supports the needs of these pupils: all schools have duties under the Equality Act 2010 towards individual disabled children and young people:

> [Schools] must make reasonable adjustments, including the provision of auxiliary aids and services for disabled children, to prevent them being put at a substantial disadvantage. These duties are anticipatory – they require thought to be given in advance to what disabled children and young people might require and what adjustments might need to be made to prevent that disadvantage. Schools also have wider duties to prevent discrimination, to promote equality of opportunity and to foster good relations.
>
> (Special Education Needs and Disability Code of Practice, 2014: 93)

This should ensure that careful planning takes place in order to provide the correct equipment, specialist support and appropriate access to the curriculum for pupils with a hearing or visual impairment.

The document 'Care and Support for Deafblind Children and Adults Policy Guidance' (2014) gives guidance to local authorities on providing services to meet the needs of the deafblind.

To ensure that pupils with a visual or hearing impairment have good access to the curriculum, *Teachers' Standards* (Department of Education, 2012) states that a teacher must:

Set goals that stretch and challenge pupils of all backgrounds, abilities and dispositions ...

Adapt teaching to respond to the strengths and needs of all pupils:

- know when and how to differentiate appropriately, using approaches which enable pupils to be taught effectively
- have a clear understanding of the needs of all pupils, including those with special educational needs; those of high ability; those with English as an additional language; those with disabilities and be able to use and evaluate distinctive teaching approaches to engage and support them.

Part A

Supporting children with a hearing impairment

1 What is deafness?

Hearing impairment, or deafness, is when the hearing is affected by a condition or injury. Some people are born with a hearing loss while others may develop it as they get older. Most commonly, hearing loss happens with age or is caused by loud noises.

In this book, the term 'deaf' refers to any level of hearing loss.

Conductive deafness is when sound cannot pass efficiently through the outer and middle ear to the cochlea and auditory nerve. Conductive deafness in children is often caused by 'glue ear'. This condition can lead to a fluctuating hearing loss. This affects about one in five children at any time. Glue ear is a build-up of fluid in the middle ear. For most children, the glue ear clears up by itself and does not need any treatment. For some children with continuing or severe glue ear, hearing aids may be offered or the child may need surgery to insert tiny plastic tubes called *grommets* into the ear-drums. They allow air to circulate in the middle ear and help to stop fluid building up.

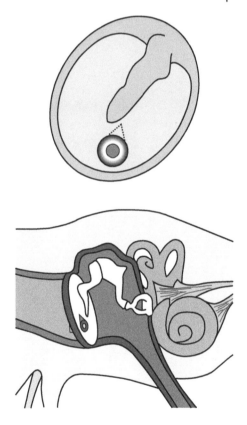

Further information about glue ear and various treatments is available from the National Deaf Children's Society (NDCS).

Sensori-neural (or nerve) deafness is when there is a fault in the inner ear usually because the hair cells in the cochlea or auditory (hearing) nerve are not working properly. Sensori-neural deafness is permanent. Children who have a sensori-neural deafness can have conductive problems in addition. This type of loss is known as *mixed deafness*.

2   Causes of deafness

There are many reasons why a child can be born deaf or become deaf early in life. It is not always possible to identify the reason, but parents may be offered further tests to try to establish the cause of the deafness.

About half the deaf children born in the UK every year are deaf because of a genetic (inherited) problem. Deafness can occur in families, even though there appears to be no family history of deafness. For some children the gene that caused the deafness may also cause other disabilities or health problems.

Deafness is a feature of certain syndromes, such as Waardenburg, Turner, Down's, Treacher Collins and Goldenhar syndromes.

Deafness can also be caused by complications during pregnancy. Infections such as rubella, cytomegalovirus (CMV), toxoplasmosis and herpes can lead to a child being born deaf. There is also a range of medicines, known as ototoxic drugs, which can damage a baby's hearing system before birth.

Being born prematurely can increase the risk of a child being or becoming deaf. Premature babies can be prone to infections that can lead to deafness. Severe jaundice or a lack of oxygen at some point can also cause deafness. Infections during early childhood, such as meningitis, measles and mumps, can be responsible for a child becoming deaf. An injury to the head or exposure to loud noise can also damage the hearing system.

As can be seen above, the causes of hearing loss are numerous. However, for many the cause is unknown. It may be from birth, have a genetic origin or develop later as a result of an illness or accident. There are various degrees of loss, and depending on severity they are classified as mild, moderate, severe or profound.

Where a hearing loss occurs before speech and language have developed, the impact on language acquisition will depend on its severity. Social and emotional development may also be delayed. It is important that there is early diagnosis so that positive, early intervention (such as the use of hearing aids and the support of a teacher of the deaf) can begin.

Where the loss occurs after the acquisition of language, the impact may not be so severe. However, there may still be emotional trauma and the need for social adjustment.

3   Levels of deafness

Mild hearing loss

Definition

An average loss of no more than 40dB in the better ear. It may be permanent or temporary. A normal voice may be heard as a whisper.

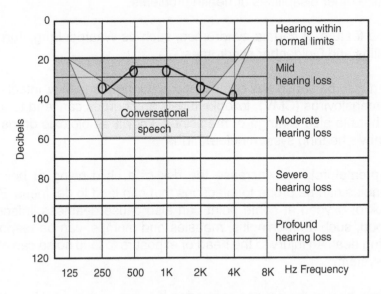

A mild hearing loss as shown in a right ear

Implications

- This loss may go undetected as speech can be heard but it can be muffled.
- There may be difficulties in understanding speech in noisy environments.
- Where speech is misunderstood, this can cause confusion and lead to a breakdown in communication.

Strategies that should help

- A hearing aid may be prescribed but the disadvantages may outweigh the advantages.
- Background noise should be kept to a minimum.

- Advice from a teacher of the deaf.
- The development of appropriate communication skills.
- Deaf awareness training.
- Regular audiological reviews to monitor the hearing loss.

Moderate hearing loss

Definition

An average loss of between 41dB and 70dB in the better ear. A loud voice may be heard as a whisper.

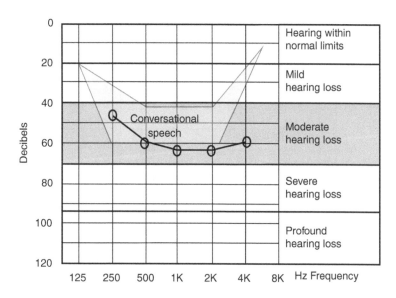

A moderate hearing loss as shown in a right ear

Implications

- The implications will depend on the age of onset and diagnosis. If it is from birth, there may be delayed language development.
- When listening to speech, all sounds may not be heard.
- Speech may lack clarity because of an inability to hear sounds clearly.
- There may be gaps in vocabulary and general knowledge.
- The loss may go undetected or the implications not fully appreciated if the person has good lip-reading skills and coping strategies.

Strategies that should help

- A hearing aid/s will probably be provided but they will not return hearing to normal.
- Occasionally a radio aid system will be provided for use in a school or learning situation.
- Advice and support from a teacher of the deaf.
- In class, a seating position where children are able to see the teacher's face clearly whilst at the same time being able to see peers.
- The development of appropriate communication skills.
- Deaf awareness training.

- Speech therapy may be recommended.
- Regular audiological reviews to monitor the hearing loss.

Severe hearing loss

Definition

An average loss of between 71dB and 95dB in the better ear. Speech sounds will not be heard without amplification.

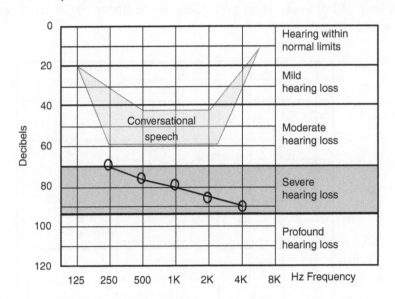

A severe hearing loss as shown in a right ear

Implications

- The implications will depend on the age of onset and time of diagnosis. If the loss was from birth and/or late diagnosis, there may be severely delayed language development. There will be little spoken language acquired naturally without intervention.
- Speech may be unclear with omissions and unnatural rhythms.
- There may be difficulties acquiring new language and vocabulary.
- Acquiring early literacy skills may be difficult.
- There may be breakdowns in communication on both sides because of an inability to understand what is being said.
- There may be difficulties understanding situations and what is expected, resulting in frustration and temper tantrums in young children.
- There may be a need to rely on visual clues.
- Sign language may be considered as the method of communication.

Strategies that should help

- Hearing aids will be provided but hearing will not return to normal; they should be worn at all times.
- A cochlear implant may be considered.
- A radio aid system may be provided for use in a school or learning situation.

8

- Consideration may be given to a placement in a Resource Base for deaf pupils attached to a mainstream school.
- Advice and support from a teacher of the deaf from diagnosis and continuing throughout education.
- Speech therapy is likely to be recommended.

Profound hearing loss

Definition

An average loss of greater than 96dB in the better ear. Only the very loudest sound will be heard without amplification.

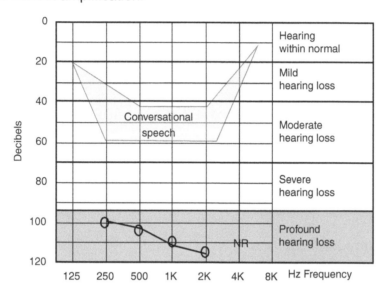

A profound hearing loss as shown in a right ear

Implications

- The implications will depend on the age of onset and time of diagnosis. If the loss was from birth and/or late diagnosis, there may be severely delayed language development. There will be little spoken language acquired naturally without intervention.
- Speech development will probably be severely delayed and it may be difficult to understand.
- There may be difficulties understanding situations and what is expected resulting in frustration and temper tantrums in young children.
- Vocabulary and general knowledge will be restricted.
- Acquiring early literacy skills will be difficult.
- There may be breakdowns in communication on both sides because of an inability to understand what is being said.
- There are safety implications especially in hazardous situations such as crossing the road.
- There may be difficulties learning socially acceptable behaviour because of problems understanding what is expected.

- Concentrating on oral communication will be very tiring.
- There will be a need to rely on visual clues.
- Sign language may be considered as the method of communication.

Strategies that should help

- Hearing aids will be provided but will not return hearing to normal. They should be worn at all times but may give limited benefit.
- A cochlear implant may be considered.
- A radio aid system may be provided for use in a school or learning situation.
- Consideration may be given to a placement in a Resource Base for deaf pupils attached to a mainstream school. This may be a Total Communication facility where sign language is used.
- Advice and support from a teacher of the deaf from diagnosis and continuing throughout education.
- Speech therapy is likely to be recommended.
- The development of appropriate communication skills.
- Deaf awareness training.
- Communication will be most effective in a good acoustic environment with the minimum of background noise.
- Good lighting with the speaker in full view whether using spoken and/or sign communication.
- Regular audiological reviews to monitor the hearing loss.
- The development of appropriate communication skills.

High-frequency hearing loss

Definition

Low frequency sounds can be heard quite well. Mid frequencies may be heard, but with difficulty. High-frequency sounds may not be heard at all.

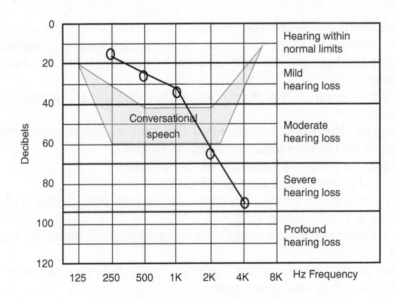

High-frequency hearing loss as shown in a right ear

Implications

- There is an awareness that someone is speaking but there may be an inability to understand as parts of the words are missing. The parts missing will be the high-frequency consonants, e.g. 'f', 'th' and 's', but as vowels are low frequency, they will be heard.
- As parts of most words will be missing, there will be constant guessing to fill in the gaps.
- Lower pitched voices and sounds may be heard more easily, e.g. male voices.
- There will be greater reliance on lip-reading which is tiring.
- Speech may have omissions of certain sounds, e.g. 's', 't', 'th', and sound 'different'. The rhythm of speech may also be affected.
- Particular attention will need to be given to the development of phonic and early literacy skills.

Strategies that should help

- Hearing aids may be prescribed but may not be totally effective; the high frequencies may not be returned to normal.
- There is a need to lip-read to help fill in the gaps that are missed.
- Speech therapy may be recommended.
- Advice and support from a teacher of the deaf.
- In class, a seating position where the teacher's face can be clearly seen, whilst at the same time being able to see peers.
- The development of appropriate communication skills.
- Deaf awareness training.
- Regular audiological reviews to monitor the hearing loss.

Unilateral hearing loss

Definition

A unilateral hearing loss affects only one ear. The level of hearing loss may be mild, moderate, severe or profound.

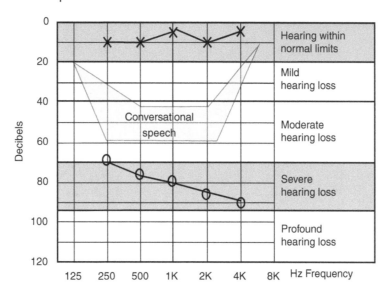

Hearing within normal limits in the left ear and a severe hearing loss in the right ear

Implications

- This loss may go undetected as the hearing in one ear is normal.
- There may be underachievement as consideration may not be given to the hearing loss.
- There is a difficulty locating the source of a sound as it is the sound reaching the ears at slightly different times that fixes the location.

Strategies that should help

- In any group situation the better ear should be towards the main speaker/s.
- Background noise should be kept to a minimum.
- In hazardous situations such as crossing roads, extra emphasis should be placed on making use of visual clues.
- Regular audiological reviews to monitor the hearing in the better ear.
- Advice should be sought from the teacher of the deaf.

4 Auditory neuropathy (spectrum disorder)

What is auditory neuropathy?

Auditory neuropathy is a problem in the transmission of sound from the inner ear that makes sound disorganised when it reaches the brain.

Someone with auditory neuropathy has difficulty distinguishing one sound from another and has trouble understanding speech clearly.

Some pupils have only a mild hearing difficulty that causes problems in noisy conditions. These pupils may be in mainstream school with no formal diagnosis.

How does auditory neuropathy affect hearing?

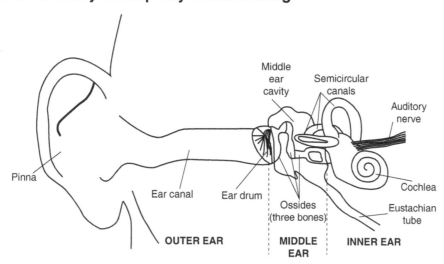

When someone has auditory neuropathy, sound enters the ear normally. This sound is not transmitted to the brain properly because of damage to the inner hair cells in the cochlea, the synapses between the hair cells and the auditory nerve, or the auditory nerve itself. As a result of this, sound either reaches the brain in a disorganised manner or does not reach the brain at all. When looking at a student's audiogram, it is important to remember that it shows the student's ability to hear single tones, but that does not mean that they can translate these sounds into meaningful speech. Some people will hear sounds but have trouble distinguishing what they are.

A few people will hear all sounds the same like static or white noise – e.g. a voice may sound the same as water running, or a bird chirping may sound the same as a pan banging. For some people auditory neuropathy improves over time; for others it stays the same or gradually gets worse. There is no known cure for auditory neuropathy.

Assistive devices to help pupils with auditory neuropathy

Various assistive listening devices may help people make sense of sounds and therefore develop their language skills. The following assistive devices may be offered to people with auditory neuropathy but may not improve their ability to hear speech clearly:

- *Hearing aid* – amplifies all sound entering the ear and can help if there is a problem with the inner hair cells in the cochlea. For some people it does not work as it just makes the background sounds louder.
- *Radio aid* – helps to reduce the effect of background noise by giving the speaker's voice priority. The person speaking wears a microphone and transmitter, and the child wears a receiver. It is useful as the student can wear it anywhere.
- *Soundfield system* – helps to reduce the effect of background noise by giving the speaker's voice priority. The person speaking wears a microphone and transmitter and this sound is fed to loudspeakers situated around the room. It is usually fitted to the walls of a room, though portable systems are also available.

Other ways to help pupils with auditory neuropathy

People with auditory neuropathy often benefit from using a visual communication system such as British Sign Language, Signed Supported English or Cued Speech.

Helping the pupil with auditory neuropathy in the classroom

- Keep the classroom quiet because even a small amount of background noise can lead to great difficulties following speech.
- Give opportunities for quiet one-to-one time working with an adult in a quiet area each day to help the pupil concentrate on the spoken words. This will make it easier for the pupil to develop speech and language and learn the new vocabulary and concepts being taught. It will also provide a break from trying to concentrate within the noisier, more distracting classroom.
- Use visual clues so that the pupil does not have to rely on their hearing alone.
- Use any recommended assistive devices to make it easier for the pupil to hear the teacher's voice.
- Seat the pupil near the front of the classroom so that there are fewer external noises between the student and the teacher.
- A teacher of the deaf can provide further specific advice for the pupil. They can advise on the correct use of the hearing aids or radio aid if used and on ways to improve listening conditions in the classroom.

5   Newborn hearing screening

In the first few weeks of a baby's life, parents will be offered a routine health check for their baby – a hearing screening test. The test uses quick and simple methods to check the hearing of all newborn babies.

Why screen the baby's hearing?

- One to two babies in every 1,000 are born with a hearing loss in one or both ears.
- This hearing screening test will allow those babies who do have a hearing loss to be identified early.
- Early identification is important for the development of the child.
- It also means that support and information can be provided to parents at an early stage.

The screening process

- It is possible to screen babies' hearing from birth onwards. The National Hearing Screening Programme is set up to ensure that all babies' hearing is checked, usually before they leave the maternity ward, or if not, in out-patient clinics soon after the baby goes home.
- The initial objective test is OAE (Oto-Acoustic Emissions) and carried out shortly after birth. A small earpiece, which has a microphone and a speaker, is placed in the baby's ear. This delivers a clicking sound into the ear. If the cochlea is functioning properly, it produces a faint response, which is then picked up by the earpiece. A poor response from this does not automatically mean that the baby has a permanent hearing loss, so the test is usually repeated. If the screener is concerned about the baby's hearing responses following this, the baby will be referred for further testing.
- The second objective test is ABR (Auditory Brainstem Response). This test checks that the sound being received by the cochlea is being sent through the auditory nerve to the brain. To perform this test, three small sensors are placed on the baby's head and headphones placed over the ears. The baby needs to be very still for this test, so if the baby is very young, the test can be performed during sleep after feeding; if the baby is older, a slight sedative may be required. This test gives a more accurate picture of the baby's hearing status. Following the test, the audiologists will make a decision as to whether hearing aids will be required.
- If this decision is taken, then the audiologists will inform Education Services and possibly Speech Therapy so that further advice, support and information can be given to the family on a regular basis.

6 Early support

When a child is diagnosed as having a hearing loss, support needs to be given to the child and family to ensure that the child is able to progress to achieve their full potential. Pre-school teachers of the deaf aim to give a wide range of advice and support to deaf children and their families.

The pre-school teacher of the deaf will provide:

- support to children and their families from the time the deafness is diagnosed;
- regular visits to home and settings;
- a wide range of information and advice about deafness and related issues;
- coordination, support and advice to professionals in early years settings;
- liaison with other relevant professionals, including Social Services, Speech and Language therapists, Children's Centres, Implant Centres and Audiology clinics;
- specialist equipment such as radio aids systems, training on management, use and in-house technical support;
- advice on communication options.

The support offered by a pre-school teacher of the deaf can include:

- encouragement to the parents to be involved in their child's learning and development, tracking this by using relevant assessment materials;
- helping parents/carers and professionals to have high expectations of the educational standards deaf children can achieve;
- monitoring the child's use of their hearing and their listening skills in the home, early years settings and the clinic;
- the offer of signed communication and home tuition from deaf instructors;
- the assessment of the child's communication skills and giving advice on developing language;
- empowering parents to make informed choices by providing unbiased information;
- fitting of equipment at home;
- checking that hearing aids and radio aids are working correctly;
- supporting the effective use and management of hearing aids/cochlear implants at home and in the early years settings;
- promoting the development of social and emotional skills;
- helping parents to access benefits relating to deafness;
- accessing a graphics team, if available, to provide visual materials to support the child's learning.

Pre-school teachers of the deaf also have a role in:

- raising the expectations of deaf children's achievements;
- ensuring that parents have unbiased information;
- providing opportunities for parents of deaf children to meet each other both locally and nationally;
- supporting the placement of deaf children in early years settings;
- providing training for other professionals.

Pre-school teachers of the deaf work in partnership with:

- parents;
- audiology departments;
- any other professionals working with the child – these may include speech therapists, early years settings staff, social care teams and cochlear implant centre staff.

This partnership involves:

- joint planning with colleagues working with the child and the family;
- monitoring the effectiveness of the support available;
- tracking the child's development using a variety of assessment tools including the Monitoring Protocol for Deaf Babies and Children, EYFS and B-Squared;
- coordinating guidance on meeting the child's needs.

Aims of a pre-school teacher of the deaf are to:

- have high expectations of the educational standards deaf children can achieve;
- enable deaf children to develop good communication skills;
- ensure parents have clear and unbiased information to help them make informed choices about their child's education and to ensure there is a clear understanding of the effects of deafness;
- provide practical support and guidance to parents/carers and educational settings on all aspects of communication and language;
- help child and parents use and look after audiological equipment such as hearing aids, cochlear implants, radio aids, etc.;
- help parents make contact with other parents of deaf children;
- build positive relationships with parents, carers and professionals;
- promote child-centred, multi-agency working.

Joint working of professionals is essential in these crucial early years, when the child's language and communication is developing, ensuring that the child is able to receive all the necessary support, thus fulfilling their potential. The child's progress needs to be monitored, shared and celebrated.

7   Communication approaches

Auditory–oral approaches

These involve using residual hearing to develop listening and communication skills, rather than using signs or other augmentative forms of communication. Residual hearing means any hearing that the deaf child has. Use of residual hearing is maximised by the use of hearing aids, radio aids and cochlear implants. Most of these approaches will use lip-reading as an additional cue to aid full understanding.

Sign bilingualism

This involves using sign language as the child's first language, with speech learned as a second language. This approach is based on the belief that deaf children need a visual language to have full access to language learning, education, information and the world around them. The aim is to create a positive deaf identity and make social relationships. British Sign Language (BSL) is the main sign language used across the UK. BSL is a language in its own right with its own grammar and linguistic rules.

Total communication

This involves using a variety of methods flexibly, such as signing, speech and hearing, finger spelling, gesture, facial expressions and lip-reading, in the combination that works best for the deaf child (how total communication is used varies, but it is based on the principle that deaf children can learn to communicate by using any ways that they are able to).

It would still be important for children using sign bilingualism or total communication to continue to use their residual hearing and appropriate amplification.

There are other ways of developing and supporting communication with deaf children, which may be part of another approach or fit into total communication. These can include cued speech, lip-reading, finger spelling and other methods of sign support. For children with additional needs, there are some other techniques, adaptations and/ or systems to support language and communication development.

8   Assistive devices

Hearing aids

What is a hearing aid?

There are different types of hearing aid, but they all have the same five key components, as shown in the figure below.

1. Microphone

2. Microchip

3. Amplifier

4. Battery

5. Receiver

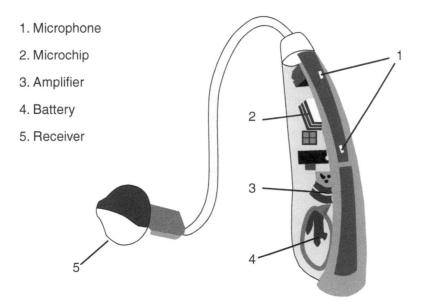

Behind the ear hearing aid (BTE)

This is the most widely used hearing aid.

- The microphone on the outside of the hearing aid picks up sound from the air as it enters the ear and converts sound waves into digital signals.
- The amplifier strengthens the digital signals.
- The speaker converts the digital signals into vibrations that then pass through the inner ear to the brain.
- A tiny battery powers the hearing aid.
- A microchip – a miniature computer that enables the hearing aid to be tuned to the individual's needs.
- A receiver, usually known as an ear mould, which fits snugly inside the ear.

Bone-anchored hearing aid (BAHA)

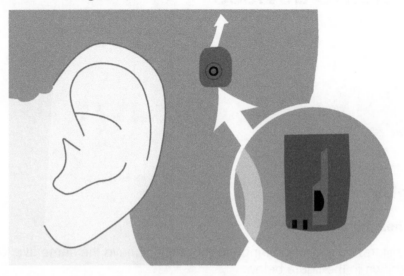

A bone-anchored hearing aid (BAHA) is a surgically implanted hearing device that works through direct bone conduction, functioning independently of the ear canal and middle ear.

A conventional BAHA consists of a titanium implant, an external abutment and a detachable sound processor. Another type of BAHA consists of an internal implanted magnet, an external magnetic spacer and a sound processor. This BAHA attaches by the magnet across the skin, without the need for the press stud-type of abutment. In very young children or when trialling the use of a BAHA, it may simply be held in place by a soft headband.

The BAHA can help people with variety of conductive problems or unilateral deafness who may not benefit from conventional hearing aids.

Cochlear implants

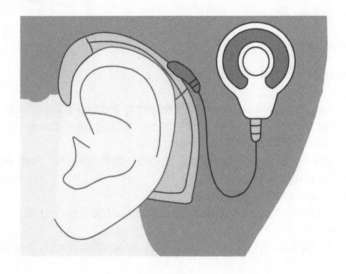

A cochlear implant is an electronic device that replaces the function of the damaged inner ear. Unlike hearing aids, which make sounds louder, cochlear implants do the work of damaged parts of the inner ear (cochlea) to provide sound signals to the brain. Only certain centres in the country carry out this specialist work. The internal part of the device is implanted surgically, where an array of electrodes is fed into the cochlea using electrical signals to stimulate the auditory nerve. The external part of the device is worn in a similar way to a conventional hearing aid, behind the ear. It has a speech processor, which converts the sound to electrical signals. These signals are passed via the lead to the transmitter coil. The coil is attached by a magnet to the implanted receiver. The signals are sent by radio waves down the implanted wires to the electrodes in the cochlea.

Intense habilitation work is required to encourage listening to sound through the device to ensure all elements of the speech spectrum can be heard. Only then is the child able to begin to process the sounds necessary to hear and understand language, enabling their own speech to begin to develop.

Radio aids

A radio aid consists of a transmitter (worn by the person speaking) and a receiver (worn by the student). The transmitter sends the speaker's voice directly to the student's receiver, making this voice clearer in relation to other unwanted noises. A teacher standing at the far end of the classroom should sound as if they are standing directly in front of the student.

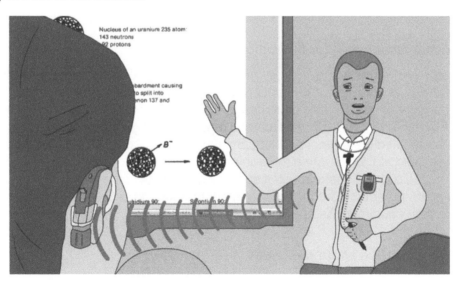

Why is a radio aid helpful for deaf children?

There are three main situations when a hearing aid wearer or cochlear implant user will find it difficult to listen:

- when there is unwanted background noise;
- when there are poor acoustics in the room making sounds echo;
- when there is a distance between the student and the person who is speaking.

Children have poorer listening skills than adults and find it harder to recall and process information. Listening in a poor acoustic environment is very tiring, which may result in delayed language skills. A radio aid will help the hearing aid wearer to hear and concentrate on the teacher's voice.

Who is suitable for a radio aid?

A teacher of the deaf or educational audiologist will normally assess the student to see whether or not a radio aid would be useful. They will look at the communication skills of the student, along with their emotional and functional listening skills. They will also look at the acoustic learning environment. Criteria assessed will include:

- the student's age;
- hearing levels;
- listening levels;
- independence in hearing aid use;
- language development;
- educational attainment levels;
- developmental levels and additional difficulties;
- social and emotional development;
- parental attitude;
- the acoustic conditions of the learning environment;
- student's views;
- suitability of the situation;
- compatibility with other equipment used.

Who will be responsible for the radio aid?

Radio aids are normally provided by the local authority. The above staff would fit the radio aid and ensure that it is working correctly. Individual or whole-school training would be given to ensure that mainstream staff know how to use the equipment correctly. Staff should check the equipment regularly along with the student's hearing aids. A designated member of mainstream staff will be responsible for the daily checking of the radio aid and hearing aid equipment. Staff should monitor the benefits and use of the radio aid. Mainstream staff should report faults to the supplier of the aid who should send the equipment for repair. Students will be encouraged to independently manage their equipment as appropriate.

Finding information about radio aids

The teacher of the deaf or educational audiologist can discuss radio aids and arrange liaison with other schools or families that have used a radio aid. Further information is available from the NDCS.

Acknowledgements: compiled with reference to *NDCS Radio Aids – An Introductory Guide, NDCS Quality Standards for the Use of Personal Systems, Merton Service for Children with Hearing Impairment Sensory Team Amplification Systems Policy Guidelines*.

9   Involvement of services

There are many services and voluntary groups that can offer support to the deaf child, their family and educational setting.

The practitioners listed below should be there to support the deaf child and their family, and to encourage them to develop as fully as possible.

Audiology department

The audiology department is part of the health service. It can help by:

- carrying out hearing tests;
- giving information about the type and level of hearing loss of the child;
- assessing if hearing aids will be useful and, if so, supplying them;
- referring on to other health practitioners, such as speech and language therapists or specialist hearing implant centres, where cochlear implants may be of benefit;
- providing ear moulds for the child's hearing aids;
- helping maintain the child's hearing aids;
- monitoring the child's hearing levels;
- referring to educational support services for deaf children;
- working with other practitioners, such as ear, nose and throat (ENT) doctors and teachers of the deaf, to provide support to the child and family.

Speech and language therapists

Speech and language therapists offer support and advice to parents/carers of children with any type of communication problem, including deaf children. They help children to develop their communication skills in sign language or speech.

Sensory support services

Such services (also known as hearing support services, hearing impaired services etc.) are normally provided by the local authority and provide specialist services for deaf children and their parents/carers in the child's home, nurseries, playgroups, children's centres or schools and colleges teaching deaf children and young people. Such services give advice, support and training to these settings as follows:

- advice related to education placement;
- support in applying for a place in nurseries, playgroups, children's centres and schools;

- advice about deafness in children and its implications for learning;
- language and communication;
- information about and support in the use of hearing aids or cochlear implants;
- issues relating to being the parent/carer of a deaf child;
- links to other services that can help.

Teachers of the deaf

Teachers of the deaf are qualified teachers who have taken further training to teach deaf children (this qualification is currently mandatory). They can provide specialist support to deaf children, either offering advice and support in school or teaching and working with the deaf child directly. They play an important role in supporting parents, carers, family, teachers and other practitioners who are concerned with the deaf child's wellbeing.

Services for deaf children will usually provide support by peripatetic members of staff who will travel to the child's home or educational setting to give direct teaching support to the deaf child or advice to parents and staff. This peripatetic staff can include teachers of the deaf, specialist teaching assistants and deaf instructors.

For children who need intensive support to access the curriculum and to achieve their full potential, a placement in a Resource Base (sometimes known as a Hearing Impaired Unit or Sensory Resource Base) may be recommended. This base is located in a primary or secondary school, with a department of specialist staff dedicated to supporting the deaf children within the mainstream school. The teachers of the deaf within the base facilitate inclusion for each deaf child. This may be through:

- integration, with or without support;
- discrete small groups taught by a teacher of the deaf tailored to the specific needs of the deaf child;
- reverse integration groups where deaf and hearing children are taught together in the more favourable acoustic conditions of the base.

The main aims of these bases are to provide specialist resources to improve the language levels of deaf pupils in addition to developing their learning and life skills, enabling them to access the curriculum and the wider learning opportunities available to them. Developing language and communication skills improves the pupils' self-esteem and confidence, preparing each pupil for life within and without the school setting.

Deaf role models

Using deaf role models can help deaf pupils to understand any feelings of isolation, resolve wellbeing issues and promote the understanding of a deaf person's rights in society.

Having contact with an adult who is also deaf can help a deaf child to learn about what it is like growing up in a hearing environment. They would be able to ask questions about being deaf, and develop strategies for becoming an independent and confident communicator in unfamiliar or difficult situations.

Deaf role models can foster more positive attitudes towards deafness from teachers and pupils. They also help to ensure that making 'reasonable adjustments' is at the forefront of the education agenda. In addition, someone from a deaf cultural background can bring valuable information regarding deaf culture, contacts and community.

Social services

Social services are part of the local authority. Parents/carers of a deaf child may ask them to assess the needs of the child within the family. Social services in the area may provide:

- equipment for the child;
- sign language classes (sometimes called language aid schemes);
- information on useful local organisations;
- play schemes and play care services;
- parent/carer groups;
- advice on welfare and benefits, and access to social housing;
- cultural forms of support.

Additional needs

If a child has more than one additional need, the family may be in contact with other practitioners and services. Even when deaf children have severe and complex additional needs, it is still important that their deafness needs are met and that support is received from all relevant practitioners. If deafness is not noticed or managed, it can cause or contribute to speech or language delays and difficulties learning, reading and communicating, as well as behaviour that is challenging.

10 Emotional implications of deafness

One in three people over the age of 60 have hearing loss, making it one of the most common conditions affecting older adults. Although most adults wait an average of 5–15 years before seeking help for their hearing loss, there are compelling reasons why one should act earlier. The sooner help is given for the hearing loss, the easier it will be for the brain to use the auditory pathways it has developed for processing sound.

The same is true for children with untreated hearing loss. Research tells that babies whose hearing impairment is detected and treated by the time they are six months old are more likely to learn essential speech and language skills than children whose hearing impairment goes undetected.

Socially, children and adults with untreated hearing loss are at risk of developing a number of challenges described below.

- *Communication*. Adults with hearing loss have difficulty participating in conversations at work, home and in social situations. Children with hearing loss, especially those younger than six months, have difficulty learning important language skills that normal hearing children learn by listening to language spoken by family members.
- *Isolation*. Adults typically distance themselves from family and friends because it is too difficult to hear and participate in the conversation. Children are often isolated from their peers or become withdrawn because they have difficulty communicating or are embarrassed by their hearing loss.
- *Family relationships*. Children with hearing loss often have trouble articulating their feelings, which makes communication frustrating for family members. Family members who have loved ones with untreated hearing loss say they sometimes experience feelings of frustration, annoyance and sadness.
- *Psychological effects*. Untreated hearing loss for children can include increased outbursts of anger, low self-confidence, frustration, embarrassment and depression. They also may feel more fatigued, as the struggle to hear and understand can be physically exhausting.

Fortunately, most of these issues are resolved once the hearing impairment is treated effectively. Children whose hearing impairment is detected and treated early can develop speech and language skills at the same rate as their normal hearing peers, which positively affects self-esteem, social interaction with peers and academic success.

11 Educational access for pupils with hearing loss

It has been estimated that over 10 per cent of school children in Britain may have some degree of deafness ranging from mild to profound. It is important that there is a whole-school commitment to make sure that a deaf pupil has equal opportunity to participate in every aspect of school life. The strategies outlined below enable the majority of deaf pupils to do so.

General considerations

Staff can improve pupils' access to the curriculum by:

- standing still and facing the deaf pupil when speaking;
- speaking clearly and in full sentences;
- being close to the deaf pupil when speaking;
- using visual aids;
- writing new vocabulary and pertinent points on the board;
- repeating other pupils' questions and answers;
- indicating who is speaking;
- identifying the next speaker;
- making sure only one person speaks at a time;
- writing on the board then turning to address the class;
- gaining the pupil's attention before speaking to them or to the class;
- rephrasing information if they do not understand;
- checking that news and information has been heard and understood, e.g. from assembly;
- reading and speaking without covering or obstructing the face;
- writing homework on the board;
- reviewing, summarising or repeating the main points.

Seating position

Deaf pupils benefit from being able to see the speaker's face clearly to supplement what they hear. This can be promoted by:

- seating the pupil near to the front of the class;
- seating them slightly to one side so that other pupils' responses can be more easily followed;
- seating the pupil away from extraneous noise, e.g. fan-assisted heating;

- encouraging the pupil to be responsible for choosing an appropriate seating position;
- using a circular seating arrangement in class discussions to help all pupils follow and join in;
- ensuring that any adult support worker has an appropriate seating position that does not obstruct any pupil's view;
- allowing deaf pupils to sit with a peer to avoid isolation;
- permitting pupils to sit near the front of the hall in assembly;
- seating small discussion groups in the quietest possible environment, as shown in the figure below.

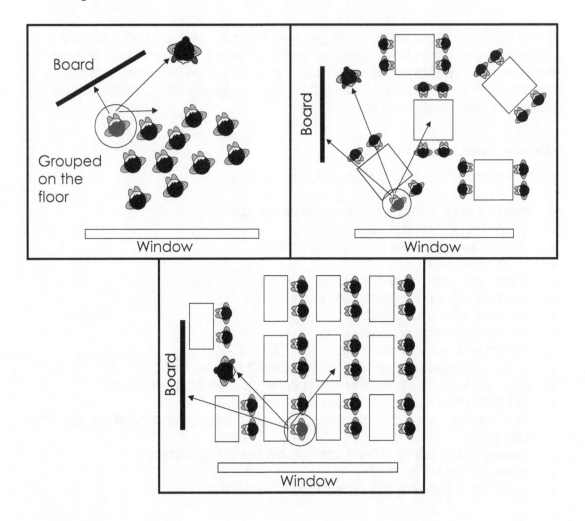

Acoustics

A good acoustic environment is beneficial to all pupils and essential for deaf students. Hearing aids amplify all sounds, wanted and unwanted. Classrooms can be acoustically improved by:

- carpeting the floor;
- putting rubber ends on chair legs (scraping chairs are particularly noisy);
- fitting curtains and other soft furnishings;

28

- lowering ceilings in older buildings;
- fitting blinds and acoustic tiles;
- taking measures to minimise external noise by closing doors and windows;
- keeping general classroom noise to a minimum;
- installing sound field systems.

Lighting

Good lighting conditions are necessary for lip-reading. This can be achieved by:

- making sure that the normal teaching position is with the light on the face, i.e. not standing in front of the window;
- making sure the lights are switched on in poor lighting conditions;
- closing blinds in bright sunlight.

Audio-visual media

Maximise the benefits from audio-visual resources by:

- sitting the pupil close to TV or sound source;
- using subtitled material where possible;
- allowing the pupil to take the video/tape/DVD home to review;
- previewing or reviewing the video/tape/DVD with a support teacher or teaching assistant;
- providing the pupil with written information about the content of the video/tape/DVD;
- using a direct input lead from the radio aid to TV, computer and smartboard where appropriate;
- having a clear sound signal from any speakers.

Additional points to consider

- Deaf awareness training for staff and pupils is vital and ongoing.
- No two deaf pupils are the same.
- Deaf pupils find it difficult to carry out 'listen and do' tasks simultaneously, e.g. spelling tests, mental maths work and following instructions in the use of ICT equipment. A slightly slower pace may be necessary, allowing them to 'look, think and then do' before looking back up for the next part of the task.
- Check that information has been understood by asking 'what', 'how', 'where' etc. rather than 'Do you understand?'
- Sudden changes of topic and jokes can often confuse.
- Some pupils like to watch what others are doing before starting themselves and often need lots of reassurance. Long periods of lip-reading, listening and watching are very tiring and difficult, particularly towards the end of the day.
- For younger pupils, a home/school book can be very useful for positive comments and information.
- Many deaf pupils are transported to school via taxis. Arrangements will need to be made for such pupils to be included in non-curricular activities or homework clubs etc. should they wish to participate.

- Deaf pupils benefit from having the opportunity to be educated alongside a deaf peer group, to lift feelings of isolation and frustration.
- Deaf pupils benefit from being supported by or having contact with deaf role models.
- When new buildings are being planned, consideration must be given to providing a good acoustic environment.

Appendices

The photocopiable resources in Appendices A.1 (pupil observation form), A.2 (pupil access evaluation form) and A.3 (improving room acoustics) may also be helpful in assessing the arrangements for a deaf pupil within the mainstream school.

12 Teaching phonics to deaf pupils

Deaf pupils can access phonics teaching but some adjustments may need to be made. The teacher of the deaf will be able to advise about the individual child's hearing loss and how this will impact on the learning of phonics.

It is important to consider the overall language levels of the child as well as their understanding of the vocabulary being used. Many deaf children have a restricted vocabulary, so teaching needs to be aimed at extending their overall vocabulary; at the same time, care must be taken that the child understands the words that are being worked on in phonics sessions.

The best possible access to sound is especially important during the phonics session. The following factors will need to be taken into consideration.

The learning environment

It is important to provide the quietest working environment for the deaf child. This is particularly important during phonics teaching. Where the class is split into groups, the group with the deaf child needs to be in a quiet room, away from other groups or background noise. Within the group, the deaf child needs to be seated appropriately with a clear view of the speaker and good lighting.

Hearing technology

The deaf child may be using hearing aids or cochlear implants and may also use a radio aid. It is important that the aids are checked to ensure that they are working properly before the start of the session and that staff understand how to use the radio aid. The teacher of the deaf will be able to advise.

Using published phonics programmes

There are a number of programmes available, all of which can be used with the deaf pupil. However, some flexibility may be necessary to aid the deaf child's access to the programme.

- Some pupils may need to continue with the listening type activities from phase one even though they are accessing teaching at phase two. Phonics teaching relies on good auditory memory which may not be well developed in the deaf pupil.

- It is important to work on phonological awareness before embarking on phoneme–grapheme correspondence.
- Some sounds will be easier for the deaf pupil to access. Most programmes start with a group of sounds including 's' and 't', which may not be the best starting point for a deaf child as they are soft, high-frequency sounds which will be difficult to hear. Discuss this with the teacher of the deaf.
- The deaf pupil may struggle to blend and segment words. Consonant blends, such as 'br' or 'st', can often be an issue. Extra practice may be needed over a longer period of time.
- A good deal of re-cap and repetition may be necessary for the deaf pupil. Opportunities to practise skills in a quiet session will be helpful.

Visual cueing systems

A specific hand movement or action accompanies each individual sound as it is spoken. The most well-known system is Jolly Phonics. Any multi-sensory approach can be a great help to deaf pupils, reinforcing the auditory learning through visual and tactile experiences. Other, more specific programmes use the hand movements and lips to indicate how the sound is made or how it links to its letter (grapheme). A teacher of the deaf or speech and language therapist can offer more advice.

Multi-sensory learning

In addition to the above, a range of experiences should be offered including tactile and visual activities. Examples include:

- 3D letter shapes to feel and follow with the finger whilst saying the sound;
- sand trays in which to draw the letters, again whilst saying the sound;
- picture cues to support the words being used during the session;
- phoneme frames or sound buttons are helpful to clue in the child as to how many phonemes they need to identify when segmenting words.

13 Teaching modern foreign languages (MFL)

Implementing the general advice provided in Chapter 11, 'Educational access for pupils with hearing loss', may be sufficient to meet the needs of some pupils. However, many pupils with hearing losses may experience difficulties with specific aspects of the MFL curriculum. This may be because what they hear is unclear or because the concept or word is not known to them in English, e.g. town hall or butcher. The use of visual clues is very important, even up to Year 11.

The following suggestions will be helpful in overcoming some of the frequently occurring problems.

Listening

Listening in class to the teacher and other pupils

- Position the pupil at the front of the class to one side so they can clearly hear and see the teacher and turn to see the rest of the class.
- It is very difficult to hear sounds from behind. Repeating other pupils' responses not only enables pupils with hearing loss to hear the target language clearly, but also stops them repeating something which has already been said and avoids them looking foolish.
- Listening and lip-reading for a long period of time is very tiring. Short sessions are more helpful.
- Pupils with hearing loss are likely to need written clues to aid listening at an earlier stage.
- In listening exercises requiring a written response, the pupil may need to look and lip-read before being able to record the answer. Check the pupil is ready before continuing.
- Give the question number each time so that the pupil does not get lost, enabling them to follow more easily.
- Working on role-play and practising conversations in pairs in class can result in a noisy working environment. Pupils with hearing loss find it very difficult to follow and contribute in poor listening environments. It may be necessary to allow a pair or small group of students to work outside the room or in an adjacent room where it is quieter.
- Listening to role-play prepared in small groups is easier if they are delivered from the front of the class where the pupil can lip-read.
- Recording all tasks and homework on the board will save confusion.

Listening to recorded material

- Allow the pupil to listen in a quiet room with good acoustics.
- Position the pupil at the front of the class and near the speakers, where they can clearly hear and see the teacher.
- Use good quality recordings and equipment.
- Audio-visual materials are not always helpful unless the speaker's face is in full view or the spoken work is supported by text.
- Avoid turning up the volume as this usually distorts the clarity.
- 'Clue in' pupils to the context/subject and the number of speakers that will be heard.
- Providing a transcript in the early stages will familiarise the pupil with the language and build confidence. This becomes a reading activity and cannot be a long-term arrangement.
- Extra practice using audio material may improve listening skills, discrimination ability and improve confidence.
- Try personal headphones with a volume control for each ear, with or without personal hearing aids. (Check that the headphones do not cut off the sound to the rest of the class.)
- For some pupils with a hearing loss, listening to recorded material is impossible. Arrangements will need to be made to have transcripts read to them. At GCSE level, pupils can have the transcripts read to them providing this has been their normal method of access throughout the course. Applications for this and any other additional access arrangements will need to be made to the examining body no later than the January of the year in which the pupil takes their examination.

Speaking

Pupils may have difficulty pronouncing some sounds due to their hearing loss. Consider:

- the sounds that are heard by pupils with hearing loss are often distorted and therefore their pronunciation may not be clear;
- always grouping pupils with hearing loss with sympathetic friends who will not laugh at their pronunciation;
- being encouraging if the pupils' pronunciation is poor;
- writing new words phonetically to clarify pronunciation;
- giving more repetition and practice before pupils are able and confident enough to speak in front of the class.

If these suggestions do not fully access the pupil to the MFL, advice should be sought from the SENCO. The teacher of the deaf can also be contacted for further advice.

14   Teaching music

Many deaf children enjoy music and many successfully learn to play musical instruments. As one deaf pianist said: 'I may not hear the same as you, but I enjoy what I hear.'

The following tips may help music teachers first working with a deaf pupil.

- Get detailed information from the teacher of the deaf about the pupil's specific hearing loss and its implication for learning.
- Research general information about deafness available through the NDCS or the local teacher of the deaf.
- Face the pupil to help them hear your instructions.
- Be aware of the difficulties a pupil may have listening to several sources of sound at one time, e.g. the teacher talking, piano accompanying and other pupils playing.
- Contact the exam board in good time to see what special arrangements can be made for exams and if any modifications are available for the listening tests.
- Find out about hearing aids. Digital aids can have different programmes put in for different listening situations, so if your pupil is having difficulty, an alternative programme might help.
- It may be appropriate for a pupil to have a radio aid to use in class.
- Be positive!

15 Teaching deaf pupils with English as an additional language

Good practice for teaching deaf pupils overlaps somewhat with good practice for teaching a pupil with English as an additional language (EAL). However, the deaf child whose first language is not English will face the combined difficulties of a limited access to spoken words alongside their individual level of communication skills which are dependent on home background.

Try to find out if the pupil is using any of their home language, either in speech or if they are able to read and write any words in their home language. This will help you understand what level of development the child is at – they may appear to be at a lower level of understanding if assessments are based on understanding English.

The pupil's vocabulary will need to be developed in a meaningful way. Vocabulary may not be picked up incidentally; direct teaching may be needed throughout all learning activities. Never assume that the deaf pupil will understand the vocabulary being used; it is important to check understanding at all times.

A signing system may be used to ensure full understanding of language and communication, either as a short-term measure until the child develops their understanding and use of spoken English or as the child's preferred mode of communication into the future.

The teaching of reading and writing may need to be highly structured and supported by opportunities to rehearse the spoken language of the task in a meaningful way. For example, when working on a particular story in literacy, the pupil may need to read the story in a 1:1 session with a skilled practitioner who can model (speak) the vocabulary used in the story, referring to the pictures or using role-play to aid understanding. This vocabulary can then be given on word cards or word lists that the pupil can refer to during writing tasks. Writing may initially need to be undertaken within a structured format such as a storyboard with pictures and space to write sentences.

Confidence in reading or writing tasks can be increased by giving the student a bank of vocabulary such as high-frequency words that they can use in all tasks alongside specific subject or topic vocabulary for that specific task. If a pupil can read the word, they can find the word to check the spelling.

It can be helpful to use a colour pattern framework to support the learning of English sentence structure. Parts of speech (verbs, nouns, adjectives, etc.) are each given a specific colour or shape. The bank of words is marked with the same colours and a coloured sentence framework is given, enabling the pupil to structure a sentence conforming to the correct word order.

Ensure that the family remains confident to use their preferred language in the home. If the child is a speaker of two languages, it is possible that they will switch between the two languages, even within a sentence. It is important to give equal credence to the two languages. The child will eventually understand the two languages as being separate.

16   Part A resources

Teachers' Standards (Department of Education, 2012)	www.education.gov.uk/schools
Special Educational Needs and Disability (SEND) Code of Practice (Department of Education, 2014)	www.gov.uk
The Monitoring Protocol for Deaf Babies and Children	www.ncb.org.uk
Care and Support for Deafblind Children and Adults Policy Guidance 2014	www.gov.uk
Pivats	www.lancashire.gov.uk
B-Squared	www.bsquared.co.uk
Jolly Phonics	www.jollylearning.co.uk
Sound buttons	Widely available on the internet, try www.primaryclassroomresources.co.uk/teaching

Further guidance and a number of information booklets are available free from the NDCS: www.ndcs.org.uk. Freephone helpline 0808 800 8880.

Appendix A.1 Pupil observation form

Name: **School:**

Lesson observed: **Class/Teacher:**

Observer: **Date:**

R   Backgrounds that do not distract lip-reader

O   Good lighting in room

O

M   Good listening conditions

P   Lip-reading distance 1–2m

U   Pupil out of sunlight not dazzled

P

I   Pupil facing text or board

L   Pupil paying attention before teacher speaks

     Teacher facing pupil

     Teacher not speaking when facing board

S   Clear speaking voice

T   Teacher remains still during delivery

A

F   Teacher able to read text and face pupil

F   Questions and responses from others repeated

     New vocabulary or important words written down

     Use and position of support staff

     Pupil given full access to lesson

W   Pupil has good esteem within class

O

R   How appropriate is work

K

     Differentiation of work for pupil

R   Microphone switched on

A

D   Microphone transferred to others as necessary

I   Microphone switched off as appropriate

O   Other comments

A

I

D

Appendix A.2   Pupil access evaluation form

Do you have difficulties in the lessons with any of the following?	English	Maths	Science	ICT	History	Geography	RE	PE	Art	Drama	Music	Tutor
Seating												
Lip patterns												
Repeating pupil comments												
Visual aids												
Clear speaking voice												
DVDs/videos												
CDs/audiotapes												
Pair/group work												
Radio aid												
Soundfield system												
Other comments												

Teaching assistant support	Things that really help me		Things that could be changed/improved
Teacher of the deaf support	Things that really help me		Things that could be changed/improved
Other things	Things that really help me		Things that could be changed/improved

Appendix A.3   Improving room acoustics

Outlined below are suggestions for improving listening conditions for children. Please be advised that any changes made must comply with Health and Safety and Fire Safety regulations.

Issue	No Cost or Low Cost	Medium Cost	High Cost
Background noise	• Manage the timetable effectively, e.g. don't have quiet time at the same time as trumpet lessons which take place in an adjacent room • Work with neighbours to improve noise levels for all, e.g. ask for trumpet lessons to take place elsewhere or PE lessons to happen further away from the building • Close doors to corridors/halls etc. • Close windows to outdoor noise • Mend rattling doors by fitting fire resistant strips in/around doors • Put foam or felt inside pen boxes, trays and storage boxes • Encourage children to wear indoor shoes • Encourage quiet movement along corridors • Introduce strategies that encourage children to value quiet and listening • Turn off IT equipment if it is not being used • Turn off the TV if it is not being used – the pictures as well as the sound can be distracting • Turn off music if it is not being listened to • Introduce rugs, carpets, cushions and soft furnishings inside and outside under covered areas	• Maintain heating, air conditioning and other electrical systems to ensure they function within acceptable noise levels • Partition areas with walls, curtains or doors • Put down carpets, including corridors and communal areas • Replace poorly fitted or lightweight internal doors with a more robust door • Line partition curtains with acoustic fabric • Put acoustic tiles on high ceilings • Change curtains for vertical blinds, and keep them closed or at an angle to let light in	• Replace single glazed window with double glazed or triple glazed window if the noise is persistent. This can be internal as well as external • Lower high ceilings

- Purchase a Soundfield System. This is where good quality speakers are placed strategically around the room and the teacher/speaker wears a microphone while they are speaking to the whole class. Their slightly amplified speech fills the room so everyone can hear equally and the teacher does not have to raise their voice. It is very beneficial for children and staff. It is generally not suitable for Foundation Stage due to the nature of their curriculum. More information can be obtained from IPaSS.

- Use headphones with CD stories. Deaf children can have special 'silent' headphones which work with their hearing aids
- Place full bookshelves and display boards against partition walls
- Put bungs or soft ends on chair legs. It may be necessary to change hard plastic ones to soft rubber ones.
- Sit near the children and get their attention before speaking
- Rearrange the room so there is a quiet area
- Put drapes, models and picture boards on hard plastered surfaces
- If fire regulations and health and safety allow, hang pictures, models and drapes from high ceilings
- Turn on the dishwasher or washer when the room is not being used or close the door
- If an area is noisy, move to a different place. If an area is noisy and you need to be there, try to turn off the noise or move it elsewhere
- Purchase a budget range Sound Level Meter (about £20) or download Free Sound Level Meter App for use on an iPhone/iPod to monitor sound levels within the setting
- Position fish tanks with pumps away from the quiet area
- Limit the use of noisy toys
- Put large painted canvases on open expanses of bare wall. These could be painted by children.
- Seek advice from an Educational Audiologist or other Noise Specialist

Issue	No Cost or Low Cost	Medium Cost	High Cost
Reverberation (echoes)	• Introduce rugs, carpets, cushions and soft furnishings • Put drapes, models and picture boards on hard plastered surfaces • Create a 'soft' quiet area using large bean bags and bookshelves • Redistribute soft furnishings • Put film, paper, blinds or curtains on windows which are not being used • 'Bring a cushion to work day!' • Put covers on tables • Put pin board on plastered walls	• Vertical blinds at windows are preferable to curtains which are never drawn • Carpet floors • Place acoustic fabric panels above display board level in rooms with a high ceiling • Add acoustic ceiling tiles to rooms which have hard plaster ceilings	• Lower ceilings
Distance	• Have children positioned near you when speaking	• Purchase a Soundfield System	

Part B

Supporting children with a visual impairment

17 Introduction

It is estimated that around 25,000 children and young people in England and Wales have a visual impairment (VI) and need special support. A significant number of these youngsters are taught in specialist schools but more than 60 per cent are included in mainstream education. Visual impairment can substantially delay early childhood development and learning, and have a negative effect on achievement.

Specialist teachers attached to local authority sensory services are an important part of provision for these children and young people, but the teachers who have daily contact with them also have a responsibility to understand their learning needs and know how to reduce barriers to learning. There are two significant issues to remember:

1. Not all visual impairment is the same: the main effects include central or peripheral vision loss, poor image sharpness, low contrast sensitivity or adaptability to light, and impaired eye movement or colour loss – all to varying degrees. A child's 'functional vision' is a key concept here, referring to what can be seen, rather than what can't. Teachers and support assistants should consider how a learner's level of useful vision can be maximised and tailor practical approaches to achieve the best effect.
2. There is no direct correlation between visual impairment and intelligence but teachers may be inclined to have different expectations of academic achievement for learners with VI. Most learners with VI have the same range of intelligence and abilities as their sighted peers, just with additional barriers. About a third of pupils with VI will, however, have some additional needs that may affect their learning. These additional barriers can affect a number of areas, such as:

   - the speed of working;
   - communication skills (particularly reading or writing);
   - environmental and spatial awareness;
   - social interaction, with a reduced ability to recognise body language and facial expressions.

These barriers can result in a situation where pupils with VI have to make huge efforts to keep up with their peers – often becoming very tired by the end of the day. When their progress is relatively slow (in spite of working hard), they can suffer from low self-confidence, which can have a negative impact on learning. With appropriate support, however, these learners can succeed in school and fulfil their potential.

18   What is visual impairment (VI)?

Vision is defined and divided into three main areas: normal vision; moderate visual impairment; and severe sight impairment (blindness).

Normal vision

This equates with the ability to distinguish details and shapes of objects. This is tested with a chart of different-sized letters read from a distance of 6 metres away (the Snellen's Test). Someone who can read the second line of letters up from the bottom is said to have 6/6 vision (this used to be called 20/20 vision when the test was done from 20 feet away before metric measures took over).

However, 6/6 does not translate into perfect vision and does not indicate other important aspects of sight such as peripheral vision, the ability to identify colours or depth perception. Having 6/12 vision means you can see at 6 metres what a person with normal vision can see at 12 metres away. Each eye is tested separately – and an overall score is given for both eyes or binocular vision.

Moderate visual impairment

This was previously called 'partial sight' and is usually defined as:

- having poor visual acuity (3/60 to 6/60) but having a full field of vision, or
- having a combination of slightly reduced visual acuity (up to 6/24) and a reduced field of vision, or
- having blurriness or cloudiness in your central vision, or
- having relatively good visual acuity (up to 6/18) but a significantly reduced field of vision.

Severe sight impairment

The legal definition of severe sight impairment, which was previously called 'blindness', is when 'a person is so blind that they cannot do any work for which eyesight is essential'. This usually falls into one of three categories:

- having very poor visual acuity (less than 3/60), but having a full field of vision;
- having poor visual acuity (between 3/60 and 6/60) and a severe reduction in your field of vision;
- having slightly reduced visual acuity (6/60 or better) and a significantly reduced field of vision.

19   Types of impairment

It may be said that visual impairment is the functional limitation of the eye or eyes which may involve:

- loss of visual acuity and inability to see objects clearly;
- limitation of visual field – inability to see as wide an area as the average person without moving the eyes or turning the head;
- Photophobia – inability to look at light;
- Diplopia – double vision;
- visual distortion;
- visual perceptual difficulties;
- colour vision deficiency (CVD) or colour blindness. In extreme (rare) cases, a child is unable to see any colour at all but, more commonly, they have 'red/green colour blindness' and mix up all colours which have some red or green as part of the whole colour.

Monocular vision (seeing with only one eye) may occur as a result of injury or disease: in some cases this can be a result of unsuccessful treatment for a squint. Monocular vision can affect children in a number of ways:

- The field of vision is reduced so a child may not see people or objects on his blind side.
- They may try to compensate by turning the head to one side.
- Difficulty in judging speed and distances may mean that games in the playground and PE activities are difficult – even quite frightening.
- The lack of 3D stereoscopic vision means that the environment may be confusing, especially in terms of negotiating steps and kerbs.
- Tasks such as threading needles or pouring liquids can cause difficulties.

All of these conditions can be detected by eye tests so it is very important that teachers and teacher's aides are on the lookout for the signs of visual impairment and are able to nudge parents into taking advantage of free eye tests for their children when appropriate.

20 Identifying pupils with a visual impairment

Many pupils who have a visual impairment do not realise that they are seeing things differently to other people.

The Association of Optometrists believes that up to one in five children may have an eye condition they do not know about and, when problems go undetected, limited vision can seriously affect a child's achievement in all areas of the curriculum. The following are some examples:

- A pupil who has a dominant left eye but is right handed, for example, may have difficulty with catching, batting and throwing in PE and with handwriting in the classroom.
- A pupil with binocular vision problems may have difficulty in reading.
- Some conditions let too much light into the eye, which leads to reduced vision in bright light.
- Others can result in patchy vision (a bit like looking through a colander), images may be blurred or parts of the 'picture' may be missing.

Children's eyes develop until they are 7 or 8 years old, and during this time the vision is quite flexible and can be improved by treatment (it can also get worse if the problem is not treated). Wearing the prescribed glasses at this age, and while the eyes are continuing their development, can give the child good vision that stays with them throughout their adult life. It is important, therefore, to encourage children to wear their prescribed glasses (and make sure they are clean): Harry Potter and various celebrities have made wearing specs quite 'cool' for many youngsters – but the occasional compliment from a teacher is always a good form of encouragement.

Signs of visual impairment include:

- holding his/her head close to the table and/or at an odd angle;
- holding books too close or too far away;
- needing to sit close up to the whiteboard;
- blinking a lot, rubbing eyes;
- screwing up eyes to look at things, squinting at the board;
- having sore-looking, weepy eyes;
- being clumsy, often bumping into or tripping over things;
- complaining of headaches;
- being sensitive to bright lights;

- having poor balance;
- finding it difficult to thread, colour inside the lines, cut out accurately;
- struggling to read the scale on a ruler or measuring jug;
- having poor presentation skills – producing messy work;
- being confused between similarly shaped letters/words;
- having difficulty with copying.

Blind learners

Educationally blind learners have a level of sight that is insufficient to learn visually, and so rely on their other senses. Many of these pupils attend specialist schools and colleges equipped to teach Braille and tactile skills and help learners to develop as much independence as possible in everyday life. When they are included in mainstream settings, they will usually be supported by a TA and have an Education, Health and Care Plan to detail their needs and provision made for them.

Partially sighted learners

Partially sighted learners still work primarily through the visual medium and usually attend mainstream schools. Their needs vary considerably and many manage to work with normal print, which can result in their needs being underestimated.

21 Professionals who work with visually impaired children and their families

A qualified teacher of the visually impaired (QTVI)

This is a teacher who has undergone specialist training to teach pupils with visual impairments. Areas might include: early years development, special communication skills, pre-Braille skills, sensory development, the use of low vision devices and social skills.

Following the referral of a child to a Sensory Service, an initial home visit can be arranged with a QTVI. The purpose of the visit is to introduce the Sensory Service, to seek further information on the nature and extent of a child's visual difficulties and, where appropriate, complete a brief initial functional visual assessment. The outcome of this visit will be discussed with the parent/carer and agreement reached on the need for any further action. Where the necessity for further action has been identified, a qualified teacher of the visually impaired will be available to work with parents and children.

This support teacher will become the key link between the Sensory Service, playgroup, nursery or school and the family, working in partnership with everyone involved with the child.

According to the RNIB (2012), the role of QTVI includes the following:

- Managing referrals from health, settings and families to education with clear referral routes and eligibility criteria.
- Providing direct support to babies and young children with vision impairment and their parent carers in the home to support early development and learning through play and to promote parental confidence.
- Assessing children and young people's functional vision in liaison with health professionals.
- Liaising with health professionals on the range of available low vision devices and how to use them.
- Advising in mainstream and specialist early years, school and FE and HE settings on strategies for curriculum access and independent learning.
- Guiding the work of other professionals, such as teachers, teaching assistants and therapists through INSET, ongoing specialist advice and direct teaching.
- Teaching specialist skills, for example Braille, the use of specialist equipment and ICT, and independent living and learning skills.
- Adapting and modifying teaching and learning resources in print, audio or tactile formats and training setting based staff to do this.

- Advising on access arrangements for exams.
- Using strategies to help develop the visual and communication skills of children and young people with additional or complex needs.
- Advising on and how appropriate communication strategies can enhance children and young people's functional vision.
- Informally assessing learning environments for accessibility and health and safety, and reviewing access plans (in line with the Equality Act).
- Liaising and working with habilitation workers on mobility and independence skills.
- Promoting and delivering training on emotional wellbeing and social and communication skills.
- Providing a birth to 25 service, including effective transition arrangements at key stages from birth through awareness raising, training, transfer of information and ensuring specialist equipment is in place in the new setting.
- Supporting students through transition into post 16/FE provision and into independent adulthood.

Specialist teaching assistant (TA) VI

Specialist help can be provided by a fully trained and qualified teaching assistant who will visit families of children with visual impairments to help promote children's visual development. This could include practical issues such as encouraging the development of body image and awareness, stimulating better use of impaired vision or developing early play skills. The support teacher and teacher's aide would always work closely with parents in order to meet the needs of both the parents and the child.

Mobility and habilitation

A specially trained person who can teach visually impaired children to travel independently. Areas might include: the use of a cane, conceptual development, body image, spatial awareness, directions, and familiarisation to new environments, self-help/daily living skills.

Ophthalmologist

A medical professional who has specialised in the diagnosis and treatment of eye defects and diseases, who can perform eye surgery and prescribe medication, provide medical information and advice regarding visual impairments.

Optometrist

A practitioner who can measure refractive errors and prescribe glasses; may also prescribe optical devices in special cases.

Optician

A specially trained person who performs eye tests and matches correct lenses to prescriptions, fits them into frames and adjusts frames to the correct positions.

Family doctor, paediatrician

May make a referral to the eye clinic and hospital.

Others

Other professionals who may be involved with a child who has VI include: health visitor, social worker, parent partnership worker, physiotherapist, speech and language therapist, occupational therapist, educational psychologist. These professionals will work in a multi-agency way and determine whether an Education, Health and Care Plan (EHCP) is required. They may also support transition to play groups, nursery and school and consider:

- What help the setting/school will need in preparing for admission.
- Whether extra help will be needed at school and how this is to be achieved.
- Whether any specialised resources will be required.

The VI support service should continue to monitor and support during the transitional phase into school and advise staff on appropriate management strategies.

22 Considerations to be made for the pupil with visual impairment

A visual impairment may not be a child's only difficulty; there may be a medical condition or other impairments to consider. In any situation, it is important to remember that the child is first and foremost a child, regardless of visual or global functioning levels. The child is an individual in their own right and will have a unique personality, interests, strengths and weaknesses. There are, however, some general considerations to take into account when interacting with a child who has VI.

Approximately 80 per cent of all learning takes place through the visual pathway; lack of vision may therefore affect a child's ability to:

- imitate and interact socially – understanding and using gestures and non-verbal communication may be difficult;
- move, explore and touch items;
- understand the immediate and wider environment;
- be independent;
- make choices;
- develop body awareness and self-image;
- develop gross and fine motor coordination;
- be confident;
- concentrate and persevere with activities.

In order to minimise the effects of these barriers and maximise a child's learning opportunities, it is important to encourage and train pupils to use whatever vision they have to the full, whilst also learning to use their other senses to maximum effect.

Developing functional vision

In order for visually impaired children to use their vision most efficiently, they must be encouraged to look properly and be taught how to scan and search. Training in these skills should be part of an overall programme tailored to a pupil's individual needs, and with the objective of enabling him or her to cope as well as possible in school and in the outside world.

Learning to use the other senses

Hearing: just as there are different levels of 'seeing' – from a quick glance, to careful looking/inspection – so hearing can have various degrees of attention. Seeing could be equated with 'hearing', and looking with 'listening'. Visually impaired children will not automatically listen with concentration, nor be able to interpret and gain information from different sounds. In order for them to become skilled at listening, the following should be considered:

- *Young children* can play listening games, e.g. recognising familiar sounds, picking out one sound from background noises etc. As they get older, children should listen to a passage read out and practise identifying the features listed above. With practice, it should be possible to speed up the activity.
- *Interpreting the sound environment* will help pupils to understand the world in which they live and move, and aid orientation and mobility. Many noises give clues about what is going on. For example, the sound of doors opening and closing may alert a child to the entrance or exit of a person to the room. Their ability to move around familiar and unfamiliar places with confidence can be increased through training that includes recognition of common sounds such as:
  - clocks above doorways;
  - different sounds made by footsteps on different floor coverings;
  - the more 'echoey' sound of a hall;
  - street noise heard in different parts of the school.

- *Developing listening skills* – pupils need to be able to listen for:
  - factual details;
  - the main point of the passage;
  - whether opinion or fact is being presented;
  - inference.

- *Using recording equipment* to allow for 'replay' – this can help to compensate for lack of visual support of a topic. Listening again to a teacher's explanation can be very effective in aiding understanding.

23 The early years

Communication and interaction

The importance of sensory stimulation at a young age for the development of the brain is well known. As the child with VI gets little incidental motivation to use his vision, there may be a tendency for him to withdraw into passivity or self-stimulation within his own body, e.g. eye-poking, hand-flapping. Fully sighted young children have a constant input of information through sight, and early communication with others is generally visual and stimulates further development. A VI child will often miss the visual clues of an adult's face such as a delighted smile at something the child has done. Instead of responding by repetition of that action and further developing it, the child may appear passive and unresponsive and this can in turn discourage the adult from further interaction. Carers and teachers should understand this issue and instead use touch or noise to communicate feelings of delight and pleasure. If the adult is also aware of the developmental needs of a sighted child in terms of what stimulates him to explore and learn, then it is possible to think about how to adapt those same principles for a visually impaired child by:

- bringing objects and faces nearer;
- making objects brighter;
- providing greater contrast, or better lighting;
- attaching noises to objects;
- reducing visual crowding, e.g. by presenting objects one at a time, against a suitable background.

When a child has a visual impairment the development of communication may be slow. Interactive signals may not be easily recognisable and hence difficult to interpret, so it is important to support the development of communication by observing the child carefully and being alert to facial expressions, body movements and sounds he makes. Be patient and give the child time to express his needs, interpret the signals he gives, then respond in a way that is meaningful to him.

Strategies for developing communication skills

Such strategies include:

- turn-taking games – wait for the child to make a movement or sound and then copy;
- playing action games and rhymes like 'Row Row Row Your Boat' – wait for him/her to do something which can be interpreted as 'again' and then repeat;

- copying a sound that the child makes – exaggerating it;
- giving the child some undivided attention so that he knows he is being listened to;
- tuning in to what is significant to the child and their response, e.g. the sunlight from the window, follow this up and acknowledge the response;
- offering hands to the child so he/she can tap them/guide them;
- exploring objects together or playing alongside with a similar object and imitating the child's actions;
- making comments about what is happening rather than asking questions or giving directions.

Young children can be encouraged to use their vision as well as they can by parents and teachers:

- drawing their attention to interesting objects, directing their gaze and stimulating their awareness;
- stimulating them to follow, track, scan – moving their eyes to locate and find people or objects;
- developing visual discrimination between 2D and 3D shapes;
- providing activities to develop hand and eye coordination;
- introducing the use of ICT and low vision aids.

Keeping a developmental journal for babies and children with VI

Keeping a journal can be useful for everyone involved with a child who has VI, i.e. families, teachers and other professionals. It can be constructed to include early development guidance and will enable all concerned to:

- record and share 'discoveries' and development milestones;
- understand difficulties and highlight vulnerable areas that may need further support;
- focus on early social and communicative development;
- promote vision as early as possible;
- support intervention from the earliest days of infancy (0–3 months);
- develop knowledge and understanding;
- communicate and work together;
- build on stages, promote new learning.

A journal can also be a useful aid to writing and updating EHC plans.

Note: The National Children's Bureau (NCB) www.ncb.org.uk provide a developmental journal for babies and children with VI.

24 Specific areas of learning

Personal, social and emotional development

A visual impairment can have significant impact on a child's ability to interact with others, develop friendships and feel as though they 'belong' in different groups. Children may have difficulty in seeing and understanding facial expressions and gestures, and in establishing eye contact with others – important aspects of developing social skills. This can have a negative affect on his/her self-esteem and confidence and create additional barriers to learning. Adults supporting the child can help by explaining the importance of facing a person who is speaking and helping the child to understand body language etc. It will also be important to help the child develop independent self-help skills.

Social skills for children in the early years

These can be developed by:

- encouraging children to socialise in a variety of contexts;
- recognising differences in personalities;
- participating in early years, baby and toddler groups;
- supporting joining in with a wide variety of activities;
- encouraging sharing;
- facilitating play with friends and family members;
- meeting new people;
- beginning verbal interactions;
- encouraging listening skills;
- joining in songs and games;
- helping them to recognise feelings;
- learning about others;
- fostering emotional wellbeing.

Coordination

This can be developed by helping the child to:

- move independently;
- understand movement in relation to others;
- improve spatial awareness;
- improve body awareness and build a good self-image;
- feel safe.

Communication and language

These can be developed by:

- maximising incidental learning;
- extending as much as possible his experiences of the world around him, including tactile experience;
- supporting understanding of vocabulary, expressions of speech etc.;
- helping children to make themselves understood.

25 The school environment

All schools are obliged to make 'reasonable adjustments' to the environment to maximise access for VI pupils and others with disabilities. An Environmental Access Audit of the school site, carried out by an appropriate specialist (QTVI), may be useful to ensure that the school site is VI friendly. The key aspects include:

- lighting;
- colour contrasting;
- possible obstacles and hazards;
- floor, pavement and road surfaces;
- doors, steps, stairs and lifts;
- auditory features and noise/potential noise;
- accessibility (i.e. for a wheelchair or long cane user);
- road crossings.

(See checklist in Appendix B.1.)

In addition, pupils may need time and support in becoming familiar with different areas of the school site and routes from A to B. In some cases, allowing pupils with VI to leave lessons before their peers (with a friend) will overcome many of the obstacles resulting from lots of pupils moving about at the same time.

Considerations to be made include:

- areas should be well lit;
- clear signposting with Braille/large print/symbols;
- corridors should be clear from clutter and trip hazards;
- lunchtimes can be particularly challenging;
- an initial orientation may be necessary to explain where trays are located, queues form;
- friends or lunchtime supervisors may need to give assistance or verbal directions to get to an empty seat until a routine is established;
- catering staff may describe the day's food selections or pupils may be given menus in advance to aid their choice;
- students should be encouraged to be as independent as possible, carrying their own tray (even if at first there is only an unopened carton on it);
- pupils should be part of the social activity of eating with peers;
- provide contrast in furnishings, walls and floors;
- a white strip at waist height provides a trail along the main 'highways' in school;
- highlight edges of steps with paint, rubber strips or tape.

26 Classrooms

Teachers should not be afraid to rearrange their classrooms for the purpose of improving the environment for pupils with VI. However, avoid changing it too frequently and keep in mind that when you do make changes, you will need to orient pupils with VI to the room. A well-organised classroom reduces visual and physical clutter, promotes accurate navigation and helps pupils to locate and clean up materials.

The following should be considered in planning a layout that ensures pupils can be as independent as possible:

- When the layouts of the classroom or displays are changed, the pupil will need to be informed and they will need time to explore the changes.
- Be sure that different activity areas are well defined.
- Arrange furniture to provide clear and safe traffic pathways.
- Allow enough space for any wheelchairs, standers and other specialised equipment to be moved.
- A contrasting colour of tape can be placed around the edges of tables and cabinets if pupils frequently bump into corners.
- Use colour or contrast to outline steps, outlets and switches.
- Store resources in a consistent and easy-to-reach location with clear labels.
- Avoid stacking shelves and containers higher than shoulder height – this not only obscures the view of the classroom and creates a maze effect, but is also a safety hazard if the shelves and containers are not secured.
- Allocate a coat peg, storage tray/locker at the end of a row or near a good landmark.
- The pupil's seating position needs to be carefully chosen – consider it in relation to windows and artificial lighting, whiteboards, ICT equipment and displays (see below).
- Create landmarks to help pupils find their way around the room – sounds, textures, scents (if constant) or highly visible clues can help a student who has impaired vision to move around the classroom more confidently.
- Train all pupils to push their chairs under the table when they get up, to close or open doors fully and to stow bags under tables or chairs or in an allocated area so that thoroughfares are kept clear.

Lighting

Not all students in the classroom will have the same needs; lighting that is comfortable to one person may not be comfortable to another. The following suggestions will help you discover ways to reduce glare and make lighting adaptations.

Reducing glare

The ideal situation is for light to be distributed on the visual task in equal amounts from all angles with none of it reflected back towards the face.

- Reduce glare from windows and lights, as much as possible (using blinds, shades, curtains, etc.).
- Cover shiny tabletops with light-absorbing materials – also avoid shiny surfaces on pages, desks and blackboards.
- Yellow filters or acetate can be placed over work (these can be specially ordered or you can use yellow tinted portfolio covers that are available at office supply stores).
- When choosing paper, avoid a glossy finish as it can lessen legibility and produce glare.

Task lighting

This is useful for students who need higher levels of lighting to see well. When using task lighting, light directed on the task should come from opposite the dominant hand and directed only onto the task. Other students may be sensitive to high levels of light and the lighting will need to be controlled to assist them in using their vision. Lamps with controls to vary the intensity of light (a rheostat control) can provide the additional or dimmed illumination. Lighting should be of sufficient clarity to enable the student to see materials and to perform the necessary visual tasks in the most comfortable visual environment.

Teacher positioning

Avoid standing in front of a window or artificial light source when talking to the class.

Light sensitivity

Students who are light sensitive (have photophobia) may need to block out some of the light and glare around them. Allow them to wear a hat or a visor to help reduce glare and visual discomfort.

27 The primary phase

No two children are the same and each pupil may be affected differently by their visual impairment and their own particular experiences. All those involved with the pupil should therefore have relevant information about his or her visual impairment and the implications in school.

It is important that pupils with a visual impairment have full access to the curriculum, enabling each child to reach their full potential. Careful planning is essential to support the pupil, with effective teamwork developed, including involving the pupil in decisions and reviews.

More severely and profoundly visually impaired children may require the support of a teaching assistant to ensure that they have full and equal access to the curriculum and that they remain safe. The Special Educational Needs and Disability Code of Practice (2014) states: 'Where the interventions involve group or one-to-one teaching away from the main class or subject teacher, they should still retain responsibility for the pupil, working closely with any teaching assistants or specialist staff involved, to plan and assess the impact of interventions.' It is therefore essential that class teachers liaise with everyone involved with the pupil and make sure that there is consistency in approach.

The following considerations should be made:

- Learners with visual impairment have reduced opportunities for incidental learning – include as much multi-sensory learning in the classroom as possible, such as sound, touch or smell.
- Visual and spatial concepts need more explanation; many learners with visual impairment struggle with concepts such as brighter versus darker, or telling which object is bigger at a glance.
- Social inclusion is also important – help pupils to understand the challenges that their peers with VI must meet and overcome each day (ask them to undertake an activity whilst wearing a pair of sunglasses smeared with Vaseline to induce empathy!).
- A 'buddy' or 'Circle of Friends' approach can be successful in creating a support network for a pupil with VI; peers are encouraged to look at their own behaviour towards their classmate with VI and to develop strategies to help him or her.

28 Classroom management

Forward planning is essential when providing for the individual needs of a visually impaired pupil. In order for the pupil to fully access the curriculum, there are a number of issues to consider.

- The pupil's seating position. Can he see the teacher? Can he see the whiteboard? The teacher's computer screen should be accessible if the pupil has difficulty seeing the interactive whiteboard; alternatively, a personal laptop may be appropriate.
- Ensure that the whiteboard presentation has good contrast and is clutter free.
- The pupil may need adapted learning resources, e.g. large print reading materials and worksheets or tactile resources such as Braille.
- Remember that a pupil with a VI may miss visual clues such as body language and facial expressions – be prepared to articulate.
- Keywords and working walls may not be accessible from the pupil's seat – consider copying for tabletop use.
- Say the name of the pupil first before giving instructions or asking a question and keep instructions clear and the language consistent.
- Give extra additional time to complete visually demanding activities and be aware that the pupil may tire easily.
- Responses may need to be recorded in ways other than writing – consider a scribe, sound recording or podcast, specialist keyboard and monitor for word processing.
- Research specialist lighting and other equipment to ensure that your pupil has every chance possible to achieve and succeed.

Behaviour can also be an issue. A pupil with VI may have become accustomed to 'special attention' and favourable treatment – in all sorts of ways. Care should be taken to treat the pupil as equitably as possible in the classroom, giving him the best chance to be independent, to integrate socially and to avoid being 'spoon fed'.

29   Reading and writing

Literacy skills impact on all areas of the curriculum and considerations should be given to pupils with VI whenever they interact with text. These include:

- reading resources may need to be modified into larger print or Braille, e.g. reading scheme books, worksheets and whiteboard presentations (see opposite for tips on preparing print);
- using audio books or 'talking books' on-screen;
- using bolder, wider lines in exercise books and on paper to write on;
- using a darker pen to write and edit their own work;
- using a writing frame;
- having their own individual copy of resources to view at a comfortable viewing distance (on paper or screen);
- giving extra time to complete activities, e.g. skimming and scanning techniques are challenging for some visually impaired pupils;
- giving additional verbal descriptions when all pupils are viewing illustrations and diagrams;
- following a specific handwriting programme or using appropriate ICT equipment for recording work;
- developing keyboard skills including touch typing skills.

30 Modifying print

Clarity is essential when presenting text to visually impaired pupils. Illegible writing, diagrams and graphics which overlap or are smudged, and faded print all hamper their ability to see. The general principles on preparing printed texts for pupils with VI will probably also benefit those who are fully sighted:

- For main text, use the normal mix of upper and lower case letters, as words will retain their shape making them easier to read.
- Keywords and headings should be highlighted in bold type; avoid italics and underlining as they can be difficult to read.
- Only use upper case print to emphasise isolated letters or short phrases and headings.
- Fat letters are more easily seen than thin letters; use letters in plain type, e.g. Sans Serif. Arial is a good choice of lettering type.
- Consider the colour and contrast of the lettering and the background – black on white or white on black are good contrasting colours. Sometimes, however, this combination can give too much reflection and so more muted colours can improve visibility, e.g. navy background with cream text.
- Where contrast is adjustable, such as on interactive whiteboards and computers, allow the VI pupil to choose their preferred setting; many visually impaired pupils favour white text on a black background, as it gives a good contrast and produces less glare than a white background.
- The paper surface should have a matt finish to reduce reflection and glare – especially important when a pupil uses illumination and magnification to read.
- Use colours and bullets to highlight important points in text.
- Make sure page numbers are clear.
- Columns of text should be clearly separated from each other.
- The type size requirement varies with individuals – 'jumbo' large print is not suitable for all. The print should be as small as is comfortable for the individual, so the eye can cover more letters in one sweep. Provide samples for the pupil to try out and choose which is the most appropriate, e.g.

10 pt (Arial)	Three stars and a wish
12 pt	Three stars and a wish
14 pt	Three stars and a wish
18 pt	Three stars and a wish
24 pt	Three stars and a wish

- The left margin of text should not have a jagged edge. Each line of text should start in the same place, making the beginning of the next line easier to find – this is particularly helpful for those using magnification.
- Leave a line space between paragraphs and between questions.
- Avoid setting text over images. Clear, simple, plain text and images with good colour contrast are easier to see.
- For larger documents, ensure that the document can be flattened so that the pages can easily be placed on a scanner or screen magnifier.
- Unjustified text is easier to read.
- Where brackets are used, leave a space between brackets and text, so that the visually impaired pupil does not try to read the brackets as part of the text.
- Try to keep whole questions together on one page. If the text or question refers to a diagram or table, try to have that information facing the question, so that the visually impaired pupil is not having to cope with turning over pages and trying to find the right place again.
- Avoid unnecessary pictures and diagrams, and decorative fonts. Most readers benefit from having less, rather than more, text and graphics on a page.

31　Adapting resources

Appropriate adaptations to resources can make a huge difference to a pupil's access to the curriculum. Liaise with the local authority VI support service and research what is available from RNIB and other organisations (see Resources page).

Tactile

Tactile representations can help to support learning, particularly in the early years when concept building is being developed. Various materials offering different textures and smells can be used to modify:

- pictures;
- books;
- maps;
- labels;
- models (of shapes and objects);
- toys;
- games;
- maths equipment;
- science equipment;
- feely bags/boxes;
- olfactory boxes.

Pdfs from publishers

Publishers will supply some books in pdf format. These can be used directly by the pupil to access on their laptop, notebooks or tablet. Text and images can be extracted from the pdf and reformatted into large print or Braille. The pdf provides a high-quality original of the book in electronic format.

Moon

Moon is a simple tactile code developed by Dr William Moon in 1847. It is an alternative reading method to Braille. Because Moon is based on the shapes of letters in the written alphabet, it is a less complicated reading system than Braille. Moon is primarily used by pupils with a visual impairment and additional difficulties who are unable to learn Braille.

32 Practical lessons

Wherever practical activities are taking place, consider allowing extra time for pupils with VI to become familiar with equipment being used – perhaps with the support of a TA or a sighted friend. In maths, science, D&T and PE particularly, teachers can research equipment available to support learners with VI and enable them to be as independent as possible. For example:

- measuring equipment with clearly marked (raised) scales, e.g. measuring jugs and cylinders, rulers, kitchen scales, thermometers (talking thermometer);
- electronic microscopes;
- talking calculators;
- Maths resources, e.g. number lines and number squares can be made larger, bolder and darker, as can squares in maths books – use tactile rulers and brightly coloured geometry equipment;
- science and kitchen equipment with modified handles and supports;
- a light box to help trace, copy and draw;
- audible equipment, e.g. balls with bells and beepers;
- high-visibility clothing for PE and Forest School.

When demonstrating a process or experiment, ensure the pupil with VI is near enough to see well and verbalise what is going on as well as *showing* it.

Safety has to be paramount: separate risk assessments may be necessary for a pupil with VI and a higher level of adult support may be required.

33 Assessment

Pupils with a visual impairment should have access to the same assessment opportunities as their peers so that they can demonstrate their abilities. Advice on particular assessments in each key stage should be sought from a QTVI and specific testing agencies. The arrangements are usually based on normal classroom practices for that pupil.

A pupil with a visual impairment may need the following:

- modified test papers – these are available in large print, modified large print or Braille (schools are responsible for ordering the assessment materials from the testing agency);
- extra time to complete the test;
- access to a reader;
- access to a scribe;
- rest breaks;
- a separate room to complete the tests where the pupil can use make use of any special arrangements or use any equipment required.

34 Specialist equipment

Modern technology has enormous potential for supporting learners with visual impairment. Appropriate devices and software can enable pupils of all ages and abilities to work at their own pace and often independently, improving their progress and attainment but also, importantly, their self-esteem.

There are three elements to consider, however, in choosing and using technology to the best effect:

- making good choices – speak to specialist teachers and support services, and consult with specialist IT providers; it is important that each piece of equipment is matched to the needs of the particular pupils;
- providing training – for the pupil, his teachers and support staff and his parents/carers; much of the technology in schools is used to only a small proportion of its potential!
- allocating sufficient time – to a) embed the learning and b) use the technology as part of everyday lessons in the classroom.

The cost of training and maintenance should be planned and budgeted for, as these can often prove to be as expensive as the purchase of the equipment.

Specialist technology

There is an ever-increasing range of equipment that might be valuable to pupils with VI, including:

- larger computer monitors (with touch screens);
- adapted keyboards and switches;
- tablets;
- electronic video magnifiers – hand-held and desk top;
- magnification software;
- touch typing software;
- software that translates print into Braille;
- software that speaks out the text;
- personal note-takers that can produce both Braille and print;
- Closed Circuit TVs (CCTVs) that allow access to print and diagrams.

Low vision aids (LVA)

LVA are simpler and therefore cheaper, but can be just as valuable as expensive resources. Unfortunately, they are often not used to good effect because the carer and the child have not received even basic training in their use, perhaps because it is assumed that their function is self-explanatory.

The purpose of most optical LVA is simply to magnify the detail of an object to a size which the child finds easier to see. There are various ways of achieving this magnification:

- increasing the size of the object, e.g. enlarge print, diagrams;
- decreasing the working distance – moving objects closer to the eye (using a raised desk for example, sitting the pupil nearer to the interactive whiteboard);
- using an LVA.

To use an LVA effectively, and to avoid frustration, the pupil needs to learn how to use it properly. The LVA used for near vision must be held at the correct distance. The amount of magnification and the size of the field of view decrease as the distance from the magnifier to the eye increases, so usually magnifiers should be used close to the eye. To keep the LVA at the correct distance from the text, it is helpful if the reader puts the little finger down on the text to act as a support and maintain the right distance. In order to make reading comfortable, it is best to bring the printed material up to the child's face, rather than the child having to bend over to the table: various stands and book-holders can be used for this.

Using the LVA, the pupil will need to practise:

- finding the start of the line;
- tracking along and back a line;
- moving down lines;
- scanning text;
- developing speed and fluency in using the LVA;
- cleaning and maintaining the LVA.

When using far-distance LVA such as telescopes, pupils will also need to practise:

- locating objects;
- focusing;
- scanning along a wall display or whiteboard.

Choosing the right magnification

LVA are available with different degrees of magnification, so need to be carefully matched to an individual's needs. It is also important to remember that, generally, as the working distance increases, so the magnification of the LVA decreases.

Field of view must also be considered. For a near-vision magnifier, field of view can be defined as the number of letters that can be seen at one time through the magnifier. It is important to remember that the narrower the field, the harder it is to read whole words, and thus read quickly and fluently; it is also more difficult to find the way around a page of a textbook with illustrations, side headings etc. These factors should be considered when deciding the strength of magnification, so that the size of letter is balanced by the field of view.

The width of field of view can be affected by:

- the working distance between the LVA and the eyes (the shorter the distance, the greater the field of view);
- the diameter of the magnifying lens (larger = greater field of view);
- the magnification rating of the lens (lower rating = greater field of view).

Types of hand-held LVA

- Simple magnifiers:
  - Hand-held: the pupil has to find the correct distance from the page, and has to maintain the position. The eyes must be close to the lens, so a work-stand that brings the material up to the face may help with posture. It is not possible to write easily underneath this type of LVA.
  - Stand magnifier: maintains the correct distance from the page, but the pupil cannot easily write underneath it, and if it does not have its own illumination, then shadows are cast.
  - Flat field: excellent light gathering properties, and less distortion than the above LVA. Their limitation is their restriction to x2 magnification and they do not allow for writing underneath.
- Bar magnifiers: have excellent light gathering properties but only magnify the height of letters, not the width, and are generally limited to x2 magnification. They are only useful for reading.
- Spectacle mounted magnifiers: keep both hands free and allow the user to both read and write. They provide a maximum field of view for near vision but have a short working distance, so good task lighting is essential.
- Bi-focals: enable wearers to focus on close work, e.g. reading and writing and also cope with distance work, such as looking up at a whiteboard to copy. They are not usually recommended for walking around in (though in practice, many pupils seem to manage).

Closed Circuit TV or CCTVs

CCTVs can be used for reading print and diagrams. They usually consist of a camera, a platform on which the material to be read rests, and a screen. Some systems are also able to focus on material at a distance, e.g. on the whiteboard. The advantages of a CCTV over a hand-held LVA are considerable:

- the degree of magnification is greater;
- the user can control the degree of magnification;
- this is more flexible when faced with textbooks with varying print sizes;
- the user can adjust the contrast and brightness;
- the picture can be reversed, to provide, e.g., white against a black background;
- other facilities such as line markers or split-screen (blacking out the text except for the line to be read) help the user track along a line and read more quickly.

CCTVs are expensive and cannot always be easily transported from one room to another. However, many schools make arrangements for a CCTV to be available in key areas such as a Resource Base. They can be particularly useful for science and geography lessons where sighted pupils can also benefit from the magnification of diagrams. (A hand-held CCTV could also be an option where portability is a factor, although these can be more difficult to use and may be more appropriate for secondary school pupils.)

The training skills outlined above for using hand-held LVA will also apply to using CCTVs. In addition, pupils will need to use:

- camera controls – to adjust print size, focusing, zooming, contrast;
- screen adjustments for contrast, brightness, positive/negative image, line marker, split screen facility and using the platform to move work.

Pupils often need lots of encouragement to see the benefit of using a LVA and overcome feelings of self-consciousness about 'being different' from their sighted peers. They will gain confidence, however, with practice and soon come to appreciate the greater access to written material which has not been specifically modified for them. Teachers should strive to ensure that specialist equipment does not isolate a VI pupil from the rest of the class; he or she should sit and work with peers rather than on their own or alone with a teaching assistant.

35 Social skills

For pupils with a visual impairment, the development of good social skills may need additional support and even some specific training or mentoring. They cannot learn as well as others by watching and copying adult behaviour. Their difficulty in seeing facial expressions and body language is a disadvantage in terms of becoming emotionally literate and understanding the nuances of human behaviour. They may feel isolated amongst sighted classmates and find it difficult to penetrate friendship groups, cliques and 'gangs'.

The suggestions below provide starting points to help pupils with VI integrate socially with their peer group and develop good self-esteem.

- Allocate a mentor – perhaps an adult or older pupil who can empathise with the VI pupil and be a good listener.
- Mentoring sessions could include discussion about how other pupils perceive the pupil with VI, their awkwardness in knowing what to do and 'how to be' around him.
- Role-play situations in class and in the playground – what the VI pupil might say to put someone at ease and help them to do 'the right thing' in terms of including/ helping him.
- Build a 'buddy group' or circle of friends for the VI pupil – with some preparation involved in how to support with regular monitoring of the situation. Playtimes and lunchtime will be a key element of their support. Ensure that they receive acknowledgement/praise for their endeavours.
- Find out the strengths and interests of the pupil with VI and introduce to or pair with like-minded peers.
- Encourage the pupils to join lunchtime clubs or after-school clubs.
- Facilitate social interaction at lunchtime by making sure the pupil is confident with finding their way around and sits with a group of familiar peers.
- In lessons, nominate a group of 'peer helpers' who can take it in turn to support the pupil with VI.
- Use circle time and assembly to raise pupils' awareness and explain how they can support their peers with visual impairment. Provide positive role models.

"Walking with a friend in the dark is better than walking alone in the light."

Helen Keller

"One of the major challenges for blind children is making friends, with whom they can share happiness, meaning, humour as well as secrets."

Vicky Lewis and Glyn Collis (1997)

"Making and sustaining friendships are important parts of social development."

Annie Bearfield (2004)

"Children who have friends are more likely to be socially competent than those who do not have friends."

Annie Bearfield (2004)

36 Transitions

When a child begins primary school, changes year group or moves from primary school to secondary phase, it is essential that the transition process (moving from one environment to another) is planned carefully to ensure a smooth transition and stress-free experience.

The child and their family should be consulted and involved at every stage of the transition process. The Special Educational Needs and Disability Code of Practice states that:

> Children have a right to be involved in making decisions and exercising choices. They have a right to receive and impart information, to express an opinion, and to have that opinion taken into account in any matters affecting them. Their views should be given due weight according to their age, maturity and capability.

The following points should be taken into consideration:

- Liaison meetings will be required between professionals involved, the parents and the young person.
- All those who work with the pupil should have up-to-date information about the implications of their visual impairment and their particular visual needs. Training may be provided by the QTVI.
- Information should be passed from one setting to the next. Successful strategies should be noted.
- The pupil should have the opportunity to visit the new setting and become familiar with it, including routes around the building and outside areas, and helped to understand rules and routines. This may take several sessions.
- When moving to secondary phase, there may be a need to have specific habilitation training to learn routes around the new setting and the routes to and from home to school.
- The pupil should have the opportunity to meet adults who will support and teach them.
- Resources may need to be prepared in advance in large print or Braille.
- The new setting may require an environmental audit (carried out by a qualified habilitation specialist) to ensure that it is VI friendly.
- Adaptations may be required to the physical environment.

37 The secondary phase

Much of the guidance in previous sections is applicable to pupils in secondary school.

It may be necessary to arrange for the local authority's VI support service to conduct an assessment of the pupil's vision on transfer to secondary school. This will determine the exact nature of his or her needs, inform a support plan and suggest how subject teachers can provide quality first teaching.

Most secondary schools will be using some form of testing on admission, to supplement results from the primary school. These tests (e.g. CATs) are in the main unsuitable for pupils with VI and require the advice and possible intervention of the VI service to enable them to be accessed. One cognitive assessment test that *has* been developed which can be used for severely visually impaired is the Montreal Cognitive Assessment (MoCA).

Teaching assistants

The role of teaching assistants may vary from the primary phase. The overall intention is to make the pupil as independent as possible. So, after the induction process that all schools offer, when the TA will be supporting fully, there is usually an intention to pull back, with the agreement of the school staff, from anything other than for safety reasons (science, techology lessons, etc.). Modified curriculum materials and/or access technology should enable the pupil to participate in lessons independently.

The line manager will guide this process, but TAs are able to judge from experience when withdrawal is appropriate by negotiation with the class teachers. They may have specialist qualifications in supporting pupils with VI and can be a valuable source of ideas and information for subject teachers on how to differentiate effectively. Ways in which TAs may be deployed include those listed overleaf.

38 Ways for teacher's aides to support pupils

- Preparing resources (e.g. modified activity sheets, enlarged text).
- Helping the teacher to demonstrate or model techniques.
- Supporting peer tutoring schemes.
- Helping pupils to write or word process work.
- Checking understanding.
- Providing feedback on pupil progress.
- Supporting and encouraging pupils to ask or respond to questions and participate in discussion.
- Keeping pupils on task and supporting the development of concentration skills.
- Helping pupils to organise and sequence thoughts and answers, e.g. using mind maps.
- Overseeing work on computer and supporting teaching and learning through the use of ICT and maintaining equipment.
- Helping to prepare pupils for the introduction of a new topic by introducing new vocabulary and concepts before the lesson.
- Providing extra practice/explanation in a session after the lesson.
- Supporting pupils' writing by providing subject-specific key words and correct spellings.
- Preparing a risk assessment for practical activities or outings.
- Assisting pupils with practical work or providing appropriate practical apparatus, e.g. adapting science apparatus.

39 Modification and curriculum access

The levels of modification of school curriculum materials will depend on the specific visual needs of the pupil with VI. Modified materials for lessons can be prepared by the LA Sensory Support Service and it is important to arrange for this well in advance. Commonly, papers are modified into Modified Large Print (18 point on A4) or Enlarged Modified Large Print (24 point on A3) for GCSE work. Modifications to Unified English Braille (UEB) can also be arranged.

It cannot be stressed enough that a long lead-in time is required for modification work. Whilst some books are available in pdf format which helps in the process, not all publishers have their full book list available. Load2learn (www.load2learn.org.uk) is building its resources and some trading is done via the VI Forum. Another source of tactile prepared diagrams is Zychem (www.tactilelibrary.com).

Where there is a high dependency, e.g. for Braille texts and tactile diagrams, there should be an on-site support team in school if possible. The equipment required for supporting a pupil at this level comprises a computer station with scanner and specialist software, as well as Braille translation software and a Braille embosser. For the production of tactile diagrams, a high level of graphics design package is needed and special 'swell paper' and a heater to complete the diagrams. The staffing for this level of need is minimally 1.5 full-time equivalent so that production of resources can be carried out whilst in-class support is continued.

Specialist support which is on-site and preferably centrally located enables the smooth functioning of the protocols involved in presenting work in advance etc., and also prepares for the relatively emergency situations that can arise, such as the morning paper being used in a lesson!

When pupils with VI need to have materials enlarged as their normal way of working, their teachers or TAs can often prepare these using the photocopier. Care must be taken to ensure that shading is maintained so either colour photocopying or 'photo mode' should be used. With enlargement, any scales will also be enlarged so the use of the scale to determine measurements will still work. If a 'real' dimension is required from what is now an enlarged diagram, then the answer will have to be adapted to suit.

The permissible margins of error for pupils with a visual impairment are generally accepted as being 0.5cm for linear measurements and 5 degrees for angular measurements, and these criteria are advised to be used by schools when conducting internal assessments.

40 Examinations

The exam boards (or awarding bodies, AB) work under the umbrella of the Joint Council for Qualifications (JCQ) and liaise with organisations such as the RNIB and a team of trained modifiers to provide the accessible exams that pupils with a VI will require. Papers offered from the ABs currently include MLP (18 point on A4), EMLP (24 point on A3) and Braille with tactile diagrams.

The process to request these modified papers is through the Access Arrangements Online website, which school examination officers can access. Using information provided by the VI service and other professionals, e.g. educational psychologists, they can input details of the pupil's impairment and needs. The computerised process will either accept and issue a document detailing the allowances, or indicate that the request is too much and refer to the boards. For example, a request for 100 per cent additional time allowance and supervised rest breaks and a reader and a scribe will be rejected.

Transcription of GCSE Braille answer papers

A transcription of the candidate's answers has to be undertaken by the VI Service. If electronic Braillers are used, these will usually offer a word-processor compatible version of the Brailled answers which could be submitted.

(This is not the case for NC Tests as these papers are marked by a Braille reader.)

41   Habilitation

The term 'habilitation' relates to the teaching and learning of techniques and strategies which enable children and young people with visual impairment to develop mobility, orientation and independent living skills.

Mobility and orientation involves skills which enable a child or young person to explore, move or travel safely and as independently as possible.

Independent living skills include any activity which a child or young person would be expected to be able to carry out at a certain age or stage of development.

These two types of training will often run alongside one another and will always be age and ability appropriate; aspects covered are listed below.

Early assessment and intervention

Once a child has been referred by a QTVI, the habilitation team will be introduced to the family of the child as early as possible, and make an initial assessment of the child's needs. Assessment usually includes a detailed discussion with the child (when they are able to make their contribution), parents and school staff and observations of their practical skills and abilities. It provides an opportunity for:

- introducing members of the habilitation team;
- allowing the child to be fully involved in the decision-making process regarding the training they will receive;
- assessing current knowledge, skills and abilities and identifying those which require further support and development.

Team members will also advise on particular activities which can be carried out regularly to encourage development and increase independence.

Mobility and orientation training

This involves working with parents to support their children and will be tailored to meet individual needs. Training can include:

- encouraging exploration and movement through play;
- body and spatial awareness;

- sequencing;
- confidence building;
- navigating the home;
- pre-cane skills;
- navigating the early years setting, classroom and school;
- problem solving;
- route planning;
- using maps;
- environmental awareness;
- mobility aids;
- long cane training;
- transition training;
- public environments;
- using public transport;
- interpersonal and communication skills.

Independent living skills

These might include:

- social interaction and confidence building;
- making choices;
- self-care routines;
- dressing;
- meal times;
- asking for help;
- food and drink preparation;
- money recognition and management;
- shopping;
- using public environments;
- banking;
- preparation for college, placements or work.

The programmes will be designed specifically for an individual and tailored to suit their age, needs and ability.

Planning for habilitation training

The habilitation specialist will prepare an Individual Habilitation Plan (IHP) which may be part of an Education, Health and Care Plan and will outline:

- all contacts associated with the child including school, parents/carers, support staff, other organisations or professionals;
- details of the visual impairment and the impact this has upon learning;
- findings and recommendations from the assessment;
- an action plan of support including the type of training, strategies and resources, people involved, time factors, targets, success and assessment criteria and evaluation.

42   Part B glossary

Acuity	clarity or sharpness of vision
Diplopia	double vision
Directing gaze (attention/fixation)	turning eyes to look at someone or something to which they have been alerted
Following	movement of the eyes as they keep a moving object in focus
Functional vision	the act of seeing and how the person uses sight to understand the world and to function in it
Hypermetropia	long-sightedness
LVA	low vision aid
Myopia	short-sightedness
Photophobia	abnormal sensitivity to light
Scanning	movements of the eyes searching to find something
Shifting gaze	turning eyes to look from one object or person to another
Strabismus	squint
Tracking	movement of the eyes as they keep an object in focus as it rolls along a surface or along a track
Visual awareness	alerting to/detecting the presence of a visual stimulus
Visual discrimination	2D and 3D
Visual motor integration	visual-motor integration allows our eyes and hands to work together in a smooth, organised and efficient way – sometimes it is referred to as eye–hand coordination

43   Part B resources

Calibre www.calibre.org.uk
A wide variety of audio books available.

Inclusive Technology www.inclusive.co.uk
Special needs software, switches and computer access devices.

Load2Learn https://load2learn.org.uk/
Load2Learn provides accessible reading books, textbooks and other learning resources to visually impaired students in downloadable, accessible formats. Membership is free to educators in the UK.

Mobility and Independent Specialists in Education (MISE) www.mise.org.uk

National Blind Children's Society www.blindchildrenuk.org
CustomEyes produces large print reading books and some textbooks for pupils with visual impairment. Requested books are produced in the font size, paper colour and format that suits an individual pupil's specific eye condition. They cost the RRP of the original book.

The National Children's Bureau (NCB) www.ncb.org.uk
Provide a developmental journal for babies and children with VI.

RNIB www.rnib.org.uk
The Royal National Institute for the Blind provide a wide range of information advice and resources for people with VI and professionals involved with them.

RNIB Library http://librarycatalogue.rnib.org.uk/

The RNIB Library catalogue is a database of reading books and some textbooks including:

- Braille, large print and audio items are available on a loan basis;
- Braille, large print and audio items are available to purchase;
- Electronic files are available to purchase.

Appendix B.1   School audit for VI access

	Well lit	Uncluttered/ clear traffic path	Handrails, grab rails, ramps	Clear labelling/ Braille	Surface change to denote hazard/ new area
Entrance					
Stairs					
Corridors					
Hall					
Dining room					
Gym					
Classrooms					
Playground					
Cloakrooms/ toilets					